Précis of
Thoughts on Thought

Précis of
Thoughts on Thought

Earl Hunt
The University of Washington

2002

LAWRENCE ERLBAUM ASSOCIATES, PUBLISHERS
Mahwah, New Jersey   London

Copyright © 2002 by Lawrence Erlbaum Associates, Inc.
All rights reserved. No part of this book may be reproduced in any form, by photostat, microform, retrieval system, or any other means, without prior written permission of the publisher.

Lawrence Erlbaum Associates, Inc., Publishers
10 Industrial Avenue
Mahwah, NJ 07430

Cover design by Kathryn Houghtaling Lacey

Library of Congress Cataloging-in-Publication Data

Précis of thoughts on thought / Earl Hunt.

    p. cm.

  Includes bibliographical references and index.
ISBN 0-8058-4253-5 (cloth : alk. paper)
ISBN 0-8058-0265-7 (pbk. : alk. paper)
1. Cognition. 2. Thought and thinking. I. Title.
BF311 .H78 2001
153.4 —dc21   2001035105
                                                               CIP

Books published by Lawrence Erlbaum Associates are printed on acid-free paper, and their bindings are chosen for strength and durability.

Printed in the United States of America
10 9 8 7 6 5 4 3 2

Contents

	Preface	vii
1	What Is a Theory of Thought?	1
2	The Construction of Consciousness	9
3	Blackboard Models of Thought	25
4	Connectionism	35
5	Memory	51
6	Visual-Spatial Representations	75
7	Language and Thought	97
8	The Organization of Knowledge	107
9	Categorical Reasoning Based on Conscious Strategies	127
10	Reasoning	137
11	Decision Making: Psychological Models of Choice	147
12	Where Have We Been and Where Are We Going?	157
	Author Index	159
	Subject Index	161

Preface

This is a book about the mind. Understanding the mind is a fantastically complex operation. As a result, the literature has tended to fall into three classes. First, there is original research literature, augmented by monographs about specialized topics. This huge literature is so technical that much of it is only available to the specialist. Next, there are textbooks about "cognitive psychology." Although many are well-written, their depth is limited by financial constraints. To be competitive in the academic marketplace, a psychology textbook has to be about 300 to 400 pages. This length forces authors to resort to "proof by authoritarianism." It is asserted that Professor X proved fact Y, but only a sketchy account is given of the experimental evidence on which Professor X's argument rested. The reader can either believe or disbelieve. Finally, there are popular books ranging from "How to improve your IQ" through "Left brain–right brain psychology." To put it mildly, these books oversimplify the issue.

In an attempt to correct the situation, I have written a book in which the major experiments and theoretical arguments were described in some detail. I also present alternative theoretical arguments, and said in some cases, there are interesting questions to which psychologists do not have the answer. Several of the better teachers of psychology in my department told me this was a mistake. They said students would be happier if I presented them with a clear, unambiguous story. I demurred. Any writer who presents modern scientific psychology as having all the answers is writing science fiction.

The problem was that the resulting text would have been more than 1000 pages long. This would have been unwieldy, impractical, and would not have sold. Publishing constraints are real; there is little sense in writing a book that no one will read.

So the editors for psychology at Lawrence Erlbaum Associates and I did what we hope is creative thinking. This book has been written at two levels: The document that you are reading is the précis version, somewhat frivolously titled *Thoughts on Thought*. The précis version is sold along with (bundled, in Silicon Valley speak) a CD-ROM disk. This CD contains the longer book that includes color illustrations. The book has been written in hypertext, using MICROSOFT WORD©. The text on the CD ROM is composed of READ-ONLY files intended to be read by WORD or a similar word processing program, and WORD files can be read by virtually any other major word processor.

The files themselves are organized as follows: The book is in a directory, or 'folder,' in computing jargon, that can be viewed by opening the CD ROM. It is named 'Thoughts on Thought.' If you open this, there are subfolders, one for each chaper plus a folder for references and indices. You will also see a file called 'Table of Contents.' The folder for each chapter will contain files for the sections of that chapter. If a section is exceptionally long it will be represented by a folder instead of a file, and the files for the subsections will be contained in the section's folder. For example, the folder for the MEMORY chapter contains a folder for MEMORY SYSTEMS, and this folder contains files with information relevant to different memory sections.

WORD permits the use of hypertext links between locations within a file, and between locations in different files. Liberal use has been made of this feature. As described below, the Table of Contents is a collection of hypertext links to various chapters. The index is also a collection of hypertext links. Instructions for its use can be found in the Index and Reference folder. Hyperlinks make it possible to enter the CD ROM book using two different methods, each of which is described below.

Direct method: Following each section of the précis there is a brief paragraph telling you where the complete argument, citations, and illustrations can be found. For example, here is the paragraph that follows section 1.2 of the précis.

For a further discussion read Chapter 1/2Philosophy.

You should insert the CD with the entire book on it into your CD ROM drive. You can then reach the appropriate section in the book by opening the folder Thoughts on Thought, then opening the folder for the appropriate chapter. A file named '2Philosphy' will be in view. Simply click on it and it will open in your MICROSOFT WORD© processor. If you do not have this program, open the file with your other word processor, using the "open Microsoft Word files" option under type of file.

In a few cases the file name will not be in view, but a folder with the first part of the name on it will be in view. In this case open the appropriate folder, and then proceed as just described. This would be the case, for instance, if you were looking for a file having to do with 'Memory Systems.'

Contents method: Put the book CD in your CD ROM drive. Click on the drive symbol. You will see a file called Table of Contents. Click on it and open the file. The file will be a conventional Table of Contents, with chapter headings and section headings. Each section heading is a hyperlink to the appropriate chapter and section. To continue with the example, suppose that you opened the Contents file. You would see the following:

> Chapter 1. What is a theory of thought
> 1.1 Introduction
> 1.2 The philosophy behind cognitive psychology

The underlined term *philosophy* will be a hyperlink. Click on it and it will take you to the appropriate file on the book CD. You can return to the table of contents file by using the back arrow on your browser.

I hope you enjoy this modern method of reading a textbook.

Acknowledgments

I have been studying human cognition for virtually all my professional life. During that time, and over my entire career, a great deal has been learned about human cognition. Undergraduate texts on the topic tend to give a fairly superficial treatment to many of the more complex details, for understandable reasons. I have tried to provide serious students of the field with a single text that contains the details of the experiments and often quite sophisticated analyses upon which we have built our theories of cognition.

This book has been in preparation for almost twenty years. The preparation required that I draw upon all that I have learned in (slightly) more than forty years in the field. During the time that I wrote the book, and during my career, I have benefited from the advice and help of many people. Some of it has been intellectual, some of it logistic, and some of it downright moral! An effort of this sort needs moral support.

Intellectually, I owe a tremendous debt to the graduate students and postdoctoral associates with whom I have worked throughout my career. These men and women were never 'my students,' they were my colleagues. I learned as much, or more, from them as they from me. They did me the honor of working with me at a formative time in their own careers. I deeply appreciate their efforts and the challenges they offered to my own thinking. I hope that I will soon have a chance to thank as many of you as possible in person.

I want to mention a person whose intellectual impact I failed to appreciate at the time, but that grew and grew on me over the years. Jacob Marschak, an economist who guided my work in my own post-doctoral years, set a standard for clarity of definition and precision of thought that I have tried to bring both to my own field, cognitive psychology, and to intellectual endeavors in general. Far too often I read 'theories and models' in psychology that are really slogans and undefined terms. Throughout his long life Marschak, politely and elegantly, would destroy such psuedo-reasoning. I have never been able to achieve his politeness and style. I do hope that this book will carry forward his message.

Turning particularly to this book, I would like to thank Jacqueline Pickrell, who read a draft, sat down and discussed every chapter and argument with me.

Now we come to logistics. I have been extremely fortunate to have been supported in all my professional efforts, and certainly in the preparation of this book, by an excellent support group; my secretaries, program associates, and departmental office staff. I am more than happy to acknowledge their assistance.

A review work like this must depend upon what I have learned during my own research activities. Therefore it is appropriate to acknowledge support that I have received from the Office of Naval Research, the National Science Foundation, the National Institute of Mental Health, the James S. McDonnell Foundation, and the Russell Sage Foundation. Some of the officers and program managers in these agencies went well beyond administration, by challenging my ideas and directing my own attention to work by others, in a way that has certainly influenced my thinking. I would particularly like to thank Marshall Farr, Henry Halff, and Susan Chipman at the Office of Naval Research and John Bruer and Susan FitzPatrick at the James S. McDonnell Foundation.

The physical preparation of this book benefited greatly from the assistance provided by Mary Lou Hunt, who proof read and commented on stylistic matters in the Precis' section, and Claudio Dimofte, who did the same for the CD-ROM section of the book. I also appreciate the logistic support of Bill Webber and Sarah Wahlert, at Lawrence Erlbaum Associates, who got me through the very last stages of moving ideas and text into a published work.

Now we come to moral support...what kept me going. Lawrence Erlbaum, my publisher, Judith Amsel (then an editor at Erlbaum), and Bill Webber, the editor at the very end, stuck with me for years of missed deadlines. When you meet Larry Erlbaum he may not impress you as a man with the Patience of Job. He was, and I appreciate it.

And for the most important moral support of all, I thank my family, and especially my wife, Mary Lou. They thought that the book was important, they often accepted inconveniences so that I could write, and without them I never could have completed this work. With great affection and thanks, I dedicate this work to my wife and family.

—Earl Hunt

Bellevue, Washington
October, 2001

1

What Is a Theory of Thought?

1.1 Introduction

Why do people dominate the planet? In one of the finest comic strips of the late 20th century, *Calvin and Hobbes,* Hobbes (a tiger) points out that people have no fangs, can barely see in the dark, have claws that are a joke, and as for looks, do not even have tails. Why is the tiger in danger of extinction, while humans worry about population control?

The answer is that we have better brains. But what does this mean? This book explores human cognition. Understanding cognition is a central goal for psychology. It is also studied in computer science, where the goal is to develop design principles for artificial intelligence agents; programs or robots that are capable of acting on their own as well or better than would a human. Finally, many researchers in the neurosciences seek to understand how the brain produces the mind. This book is an attempt to state what we now understand, and what we do not understand, about the mind as a result of efforts in all three of these disciplines. Indeed, a little history, sociology, and anthropology is included.

For further discussion, read Chapter 1/1 Introduction.

1.2 The Philosophy Behind Cognitive Psychology

One of the major questions in philosophy is the *mind–body problem*. How do brain processes produce the complex subjective phenomena that we term thinking? More particularly, how is it that certain physical events inside the skull, which we term *brain states*, come to refer to states of the world outside of the individual?

Two extreme solutions have been proposed. One, that can be traced to 17th-century philosopher and mathematician Rene Descartes, is simply to ignore it. Descartes argued that although the mental and biological worlds are inherently different, both are real, and each obeys its own laws. Descartes acknowledged that the interaction between these two worlds was interesting, but realized that, in his day, there was no way that the interaction could be understood.

Some modern psychologists follow Descartes' reasoning. They acknowledge that the brain does produce the mind, and believe that someday we will know how it does. But for the present, they argue that it is convenient to act as if the mind followed its own laws of causation, letting the connection to the brain come later. This is called *pragmatic dualism*, to distinguish it from *substance dualism*, a belief that the mind must necessarily obey its own laws of causation, and thus, can never be reduced to biology.

Pragmatic dualism is loosely analogous to the way that physicists think of events in the world as we normally perceive it and in the world at an atomic and subatomic level. Newton's laws of motion work very well in the normal world, while the nonintuitive laws of quantum mechanics control the atomic-subatomic world. Physicists are confident that Newton's laws can be derived from quantum mechanics, but Newton's laws rather than quantum mechanics are used to describe the flight of an airplane. The pragmatic dualist approach in psychology is best illustrated by proposals to model modern thinking using the same concepts that are applied to computer programs. Both the programs and human thought are described as rules for manipulating symbols, without regard for the physical nature of the symbols or the processes that manipulate them. This approach to psychological theorizing, which began in the 1950s with the pioneering work of Allen Newell and Herbert Simon in psychology and artificial intelligence, and of Noam Chomsky in linguistics, was the dominant view in cognitive psychology until the 1980s, and is still prominent today.

The alternative to pragmatic dualism is *reductionism*. Scientists who take a reductionist approach to cognition try to derive mental action from processes in the brain. The success of this approach depends on two things; an ability to observe brain states and the possession of a language that enables us to talk about them in a reasonable way. Tremendous advances in neural imaging, electrophysiology, and surgical techniques have given the early 21st-century scientist observation instruments that could hardly be imagined as recently as the 1950s. Scientists using these techniques have located where certain mental actions (e.g., word retrieval) take place in the brain. This is not the same as knowing how these actions take place.

For further discussion, read Chapter 1/2Philosophy.

1.3 Cognitive Psychology as the Study of Information Processing Systems

1.4. Examples of Information Processing Systems

Although there is no single answer to the question "What level of theorizing is right for cognitive psychology?" we can set rules for deciding what a right answer should look like. Scientific analysis depends on the discovery of regular behavior within systems of variables. For instance, in astronomy, one of the great discoveries was that the regular behavior of the planets in the solar system was largely unrelated to the behavior of the stars. Three millennia earlier the Babylonians realized that astronomical and atmospheric phenomena were independent systems.

What are the analogous systems in Cognitive Psychology? One, obviously, is the *brain system*; the millions of neural events that influence thought. This system is deservedly receiving a great deal of attention today. A second obvious system is the *representational system*, which deals with the ways people internalize information about the external world. For instance, the statement: *Damage to the medial temporal regions of the brain often results in an inability to store new memories* refers to a system of brain locations and processes. The statement: *Expert physicists will analyze motion problems in terms of force diagrams, whereas novice (first year) students are more likely to be distracted by surface characteristics, such as the nature of the objects in motion*, refers to a system of mental representations. These two systems represent two different, and legitimate, ways of looking at thinking. Neither is the right or wrong level. They are appropriate for different problems.

A third level of thinking about thought is the *(abstract) information processing level*. Studies of information processing focus on how information is moved about in the mind as a functional system, without reference to what that information represents externally or to what brain mechanisms are involved. There is a close analogy between information processing level analyses and the way one might analyze a computer program. Computer programs can be defined independently of the machine on which they are run, and independently of the mapping between variables in the program and situations in the real world. To see this, think of a statistical program: a set of operations on inputs without regard to the way those operations are executed physically, and certainly without consideration for what the variables mean in the external world. Agricultural economists and psychologists studying the effects of psychotherapy can (and do) use the same statistical packages to analyze their data. Statistical packages can be run on different machines. The programs remain the same.

Information processing analyses can be divided into two subtypes. The *algorithmic* level deals with the sorts of programs (or, in more psychological terms, "problem solving strategies") that people execute when they attempt to solve certain classes of problems. In this sort of research, investigators often literally write computer programs to solve a problem, then compare the way the program behaves to the way that people behave when faced with the same problem. A similar, more diffuse example is the use of mathematical analyses to characterize human information processing. This approach is most advanced in linguistics, where sophisticated analyses are used to characterize the complex relations expressed in natural language (syntax and semantics) and to characterize the algorithms that people use to extract meaning from a statement.

The *architectural level* of information processing theory deals with compulsory limits in people's ability to obtain and transmit information. Examples of studies in this field are experiments that attempt to establish limits on people's ability to keep track of a changing world (immediate memory) and to show how these limits influence cognition. A perhaps classic example of an architectural observation is the often-cited remark that people can only hold between five and nine discrete pieces of information in their immediate memory.

All these examples deal with functional limits on how people sense, hold, and transmit information. The questions of how the functions are biologically realized and what the information means are pushed toward the biological and representational levels.

For a further discussion of information processing models, read Chapter 1/3InformationProcessing.

Chapter 1/4Examples *describes three historically important models dealing with different aspects of information processing.*

1.5 The Relation Between Neuroscientific and Information Processing Theories

Information processing models were first proposed in the 1950s and 1960s, as part of the 'cognitive revolution' that replaced the behaviorist psychology of the 1920–1950 era. They were inspired by the development of physical information processing systems including, but not limited to, digital computers. Examples of information processing concepts, in addition to those presented in section 1.4, include Broadbent's (1958) presentation of the human sensory-perceptual system as a set of channels of information funneling into a central system; the idea that the central system consists of two memory systems, one for information received in the immediate past and one for information received over a lifetime; and the idea that certain pieces of information can be given priority in processing by shifting attention either to a particular channel or to a particular class of events represented in the memory systems. The ideas of channel, memory buffers, and control of processing by shifts of attention were presented in the abstract, without regard to physical observations of the brain.

The "black box" analogy was widely used to justify this approach. Imagine an engineer who has been presented with a sealed black box containing dials and meters for input and output settings. The engineer's task is to experiment with input–output observations to figure out how the inner mechanisms of the box are designed. By analogy, a cognitive psychologist does the same thing when he or she observers how people respond to various stimuli.

According to the black box analogy both the engineer and the psychologist are concerned with design, not construction. This was regarded as a temporary but necessary step due to our limited ability to observe brain events directly. The idea was captured most directly by Herbert Simon (1969, 1981), who correctly stated that attempts to write computer programs that mimicked human problem solving were concerned with the mind, not the brain.

Beginning in the 1980s, developments in the neurosciences led many scientists to question the need for the black box analogy. Indeed, the Nobel laureate Francis Crick (1994) has claimed that the black box approach is fundamentally mistaken. The reason for this shift in view, one which is not shared by all cognitive psychologists, is that there has been a tremendous increase in our ability to view brain processes directly. This increase is due to four advances. The most dramatic of these is the development of a variety of imaging techniques for looking at the intact brain. It is now possible to picture a brain structure or locate metabolic activity in a human being without invasive surgery. We can also detect and locate electrical activity in the brain by recording from the exterior of the skull. These imaging techniques are feasible because of advances in the physical sciences and computing. In addition, two much older methods for observing brain–mind relations have been updated. Techniques for the study of changes in mental function following brain injury, *cognitive neuropsychology*, are now sophisticated. And finally, advances in surgical techniques have made it possible to study mind–brain relations in patients whose brain must be exposed during certain types of surgery, such as removal of brain tumors. As a result of these advances, cognitive neuroscience is considered one of the most exciting areas of psychology.

The advances in cognitive neuroscience do not undermine the information-processing approach. In fact, cognitive neuroscience depends on possession of information processing models. Neuroscientific observations correlate brain activity with behavior. Therefore, they are most informative when the behavior isolates a particular cognitive function. It is not terribly informative to know that there is activity all over the brain when a person is doing something very complicated. It is informative to know that brain activity changes its locus as a person looks at lines, looks at words, and looks at a word and thinks of a semantic relation, such as looking at the word CAT and thinking of DOG. Brain activity in specific locations can then be related to the additions in mental functionality as the behavioral task becomes more complex (Posner & Raichle, 1994). But to know how to complicate the behavioral task you have to have an information processing model of how the mind works. Therefore, the information processing and neuroscientific approaches should be seen as complementary, not opposing, ways of studying the brain and the mind.

For further discussion, read Chapter 1/5Biology&Computation. *This page contains links to pages for subsections that describe the neuroscientific methods of observation in more detail, together with illustrative studies.*

1.6 The Argument for Representational Levels

Current investigations in cognitive psychology are heavily weighted toward the study of information processing models, biological theories, and their interaction. Some philosophers have claimed that this approach is inadequate. Their argument is that thought is about something external. It is not enough to know how the brain manipulates information at either the biological or purely symbolic level. To understand a person's thought it is necessary to know how information processing structures inside the brain–mind system represent states of the external world. This is sometimes referred to as the problem of *intention*.

According to this view, thinking is a process of extracting certain information from the environment and representing it in a manner that guides action. There are situations where guides for action can only be developed after an extensive series of computations on the representation. To illustrate, at the time I wrote this précis (early 2001), there was an ongoing debate over whether the U.S.–Russian Antiballistic Missile (ABM) treaty should be modified. Presumably, U.S. and Russian political leaders conducted extensive internal computations on mental representations of this complex problem. One view of thinking is that to understand their thoughts, one has to understand the computations that they use to explore the implications of statements in general. The particular representation of the missile treaty situation would be dealt with as a special case. This would be consistent with the early work on computer modeling (e.g., Newell & Simon, 1972), characterized by a search for general purpose algorithms that could model human thinking about a variety of problems. The logic of this effort is discussed in detail in chap. 3.

Another view is that thinking depends on selecting internal representations that highlight one or another aspect of the external world, in such a way that the problems posed by the external situation can be solved by trivial computations. Solutions then fall out of the interaction between actions and the external world, rather than by being developed inside the mind and then applied to the world. If this model is correct, our attention should shift from an attempt to find general problem solving techniques (and to a lesser extent, cognitive architectures) to an attempt to understand what aspects of the external world are represented in different situations and how those representations control action. Our view of thought shifts from a picture of the thinker as a general problem solver to the thinker as a collection of situation-specific solutions (Agre, 1997; Clancey, 1997).

A number of compelling illustrations of situation-specific thought can be provided. Many deal with situations in which a person must act on a problem as it is presented. Catching a fly ball in baseball is an example. In the abstract, determining where a fly ball is going to land is a complicated problem in physics. In practice, baseball players can detect where a fly ball is going to land by tracking only a few, easily perceivable, variables.

Similar (although somewhat less compelling) arguments can be given for problem solving that are not tied to immediate action. When people read a story they neither analyze nor memorize all the text. Instead, they develop general ideas of what the text is about, emphasizing those aspects of the narrative that they think are important. In a somewhat analogous situation, landscape gardeners and botanists think of trees in somewhat different ways, because what is important to the gardener (appearance, maintainability, cost) is not the same as what is important to the botanist (method of reproduction, genetic links; Medin et al., 1997). Therefore, the representationist argues, to understand thinking you have to understand what a person is thinking about, as much, if not more, than you have to understand information processing limits and the biological foundations of thought.

To develop these ideas further, read Chapter 1/6Representations.

1.7 Objections

1.8 Preview of This Book

I believe that we need all three levels of theory. Biological observations cannot be understood (or sometimes even be made) without information processing theories. I also believe that in the interest of reductionism, information processing theories are needed to provide an explanation of how we come to think about specific topics in certain ways. Therefore, information processing theories form a vital link between neuroscientific observations and discussions of how people think about very complex things, ranging from baseball games to the multiple levels of meaning in the novel *Moby Dick*.

The book is organized to reflect these beliefs. It can be thought of as being organized into four sections. This chapter and the next develop some basic ideas and facts about cognition. Chapters 3 and 4 deal with the major theoretical approaches in the field. Chapters 5, 6, and 7 deal with three of the major processes of thought: *memory, spatial-visual reasoning,* and *language*. The remaining chapters approach representational issues, by dealing with the organization of knowledge, problem solving, and decision making.

For further discussion read Chapter 1/7&8Summary.

2

The Construction of Consciousness

2.1 Introductory Concepts

Our society depends a great deal on information processing machines. These are communication and decision systems whose main purpose is to send descriptions of situations from one place to another. The idea can be illustrated by examining the difference between a telephone line and a railroad line. A telephone line is used to transmit messages while a railroad line transmits physical objects. One of the insights of the 1950–1960 decade was that the concepts used to describe external information processing systems, such as a telephone system, can also be applied to understanding human perception and cognition.

Two of these concepts are particularly useful. One is the notion of *channel capacity*. A *channel* is a route by which information is moved from one place to another. When a message is transmitted, the channel has to assume a configuration, called a *state*. *Channel capacity* is the limit determined by the number of states that can be assumed over a unit of time. For instance, television news broadcasts offer nightly business reports, in which changes in the stock market are described. These reports are highly selective descriptions of actual changes in stock prices, for the news broadcasters cannot speak rapidly enough to describe the hundreds of thousands of transactions that take place every day.

Although the human visual system is superficially very different from the nightly business report it is also limited by channel capacity. The retina is capable of detecting slightly over 10^{12} different patterns of light in a second, but the optic nerve, which transmits information from the retina to the brain, can only send about 10^9 different messages to the brain. Just as the newscaster has to be selective because he or she cannot speak fast enough to keep up with the stock market, the visual system has to be selective because the optic nerve cannot keep up with the retina.

The second useful concept is the *cybernetic principle*. Human behavior is often said to be goal-directed; we do things because we want a particular outcome. On the other hand, machines are mechanical. A pilot may want his airplane to fly from Seattle to St. Louis, but the airplane has no such goal. This contrast poses a problem to a reductionist, because to a reductionist a human is a physical machine, made of biological components. How is it, then, that we appear to exhibit purposeful behavior?

According to the cybernetic principle, a machine can contain in itself a target state and sensors that allow it to track its motion through some set of allowable states. The machine can then determine whether it is approaching the target state and adjust its own motion accordingly. For instance, the automatic pilot (computer) on an aircraft can be set to a desired heading. If the aircraft is deflected from that heading by air currents the automatic pilot corrects for the deflection. To an outside observer the machine appears to be behaving purposively; it is as if the airplane did want to fly to St. Louis. More generally, any device that self-corrects its settings so it moves to and maintains a desired state is called a cybernetic machine. An airplane with an automatic pilot and a thermostat in a building are both cybernetic machines. They each exhibit purposeful behavior in the sense that they are goal-seeking, but the goal does not exhibit any mysterious, attractive force for the machine.

For amplification on these ideas, see Chapter 2/1InformationPrinciples. *This section shows how two classic psychological studies on problem solving in animals can be regarded as examples of the behavior of an information processing machine.*

2.2 Information Transmission During Perception

This section applies the concepts derived from communication theory to perception of the world, using an extended example from vision and a brief discussion of audition.

THE CONSTRUCTION OF CONSCIOUSNESS

When discussing vision, we must distinguish between the *distal stimulus*, the external structure generating a stimulus, and the *proximal stimulus*, the physical signal reaching the retina. For example, if you look at a dog on a bright, sunny day, the dog is the distal stimulus and the light reflected from the dog into your eyes is the proximal stimulus. The proximal stimulus is often ambiguous; different distal stimuli could produce the same proximal stimulus. Also, the same distal stimulus may produce different proximal stimuli in different situations. For instance, if you and the dog move indoors, the wavelength of the light reflected from the dog to your eyes changes but the perceived color of the dog does not. Similar examples can be given for shape. The retina is a two-dimensional field, although the world is three-dimensional. An elliptical figure appearing on the plane of the retina could either be an ellipse on a plane at right angles to the line of sight, or a circle lying on a plane that is tilted with respect to the line of sight. Nevertheless, we can easily perceive coins lying on tables and dogs do not take on different colors indoors and outdoors. Why not?

Visual perception involves a great deal of coding and recoding of ambiguous stimulus features. This is called the analysis of *bottom-up* cues. For instance, in normal situations the retina detects the ambient light and allows for it when determining an object's color. This is why the dog's perceived color remains constant from morning to night, indoors and out. In addition, expectations and interpretations of a scene will influence our perception of parts of that scene. Such influences are called *top-down* cues.

To combine bottom-up and top-down cues, the visual system relies on progressively more abstract codings of the distal stimulus. The image on the retina is a *punctate* image (i.e., it consists of dots of color and light, rather like a Seurat painting). By the time the message reaches the visual cortex (in the occipital lobe at the back of the brain) the image has been changed to a collection of lines and curves, somewhat like the change from dots to brush strokes. These are then recoded further, breaking the information in the retina into two channels of information. The first channel goes from the visual cortex along the *dorsal* (top) part of the brain, through the parietal lobes to the frontal cortex. This channel contains information about location and movement. The second channel goes from the visual cortex along the *ventral* (bottom) part of the brain, through the temporal lobes. This channel contains information about object shape and color.

One of the major questions in vision research is what sort of "alphabet" is used within each of the channels. There is an analogy here to the stock market example, where the newscaster uses the words of English to describe changes in thousands of stock prices. A listener infers the nature of changes in prices from statements like "the market moved ahead today." The visual system apparently infers the nature of three-dimensional objects from detection of the projection of certain standard forms, such as a tilted cylinder, at particular locations in the visual field. The exact alphabet of forms is not unknown. Because we know that location and form-detection take place respectively in the dorsal and ventral streams, the visual system has to put the percept back together again. This apparently takes place in the frontal cortex, but the details of the reassembly are unclear.

Finally, there are many feedback channels from points relatively far along the dorsal and ventral channels to the visual cortex. Therefore, formation of a percept can be influenced both by bottom-up and top-down signals.

The same principles apply in audition, and especially, in speech perception. A person listening to speech in a familiar language hears phonemes, although different sound spectrums can be produced by the same phoneme, spoken in different contexts (e.g., the |d| in the sounds |di| and |du|). We also treat permissible variations on the same phoneme as indicators of the same signal, while making a sharp distinction between permissible and impermissible variations. For example, the English phonemes |l| and |r| blend continuously into each other. Try saying |love| and |rove| and note how the position of your tongue changes from forward in the mouth, for |love|, to back in the mouth, for |rove|. If you systematically move the tongue backward and if you are an English speaker, you will hear a sharp distinction between the |l| and |r| sounds, thus recoding a continuous dimension into a binary signal. Unlike coding of geometric forms in the visual system, this distinction is learned. If your first language is not English, and especially if it is an Asian language that does not use the |l|-|r| distinction, you will have much more difficulty hearing the sharp break between phonemes. The distinction is apparently learned early, in infancy.

For amplification on communication principles in perception, see Chapter 2/2Perception.

2.3 Consciousness

At the end of all this information processing we become consciously aware of something. Just what consciousness means has been the subject of a great deal of debate in psychology and philosophy. Phenomenologically, a person is aware of something if the thing (or more correctly, its mental representation) is available for manipulation by other cognitive processes. For instance, we are clearly aware of something if we can name it. This approach makes a sharp distinction between conscious and unconscious processing.

Such a distinction was contained in Atkinson and Shiffrin's (1968) influential model of immediate memory. According to the Atkinson and Shiffrin model, the sensory-perceptual system first delivers information to a *buffer memory*, which is capable of holding large amounts of information for a brief time period, probably only a few milliseconds. The contents of the buffer memory are not available for manipulation, and therefore, a person would not be consciously aware of them. Top-down processes select some of this information for entry into short term memory. Atkinson and Shiffrin characterized short-term memory as being able to hold a small amount of information for as long as desired, provided that the information was being actively attended to. Because information in short term memory was being manipulated, one would be consciously aware of it. Finally, automatic processes transfer information from short term to long term memory. This can take an appreciable amount of time. Therefore, selective memorization of information could occur in two ways: by selective choice of information to be moved from the buffer memory to short term memory, and by rehearsal of the information (or a transformation of it) in short term memory until it has been transferred to long term memory.

The Atkinson and Shiffrin model has been extremely influential for two reasons. The first is that Atkinson and Shiffrin's own experiments showed that the model gave an unusually accurate account of a number of laboratory studies where participants memorized arbitrary information, such as pairings of numbers and nouns. The second, and possibly more important, reason for the model's influence was that it is an extremely good heuristic explanation of memory phenomena both in and out of the laboratory. Consider the all-too-common event where you forget a person's name although you have just been introduced to them. According to the Atkinson and Shiffrin (1968) model, the name was placed in short term memory when the introduction was made. Now suppose your attention is diverted. The diverting information enters into short term memory, displacing the person's name before it has been written into long term memory. You could have avoided this embarrassment by executing what they refer to as a *control strategy*; like rehearsing the name several times before attending to something else.

Atkinson and Shiffrin (1968) used a mathematical model to estimate the number of items that can be kept in short term memory. They concluded that short term memory can only hold two or three chunks of information. This estimate is consistent with the widely held belief that the (small) size of immediate memory often imposes a limit on the complexity of human thought. However, the estimate seems too small, on two grounds. Intuitively, it does not seem possible that we could do all the things we obviously can do (especially, language comprehension) if we have such limited immediate memories. Also, Atkinson and Shiffrin's estimate was less than half of Miller's (1956) well-known estimate that human memory can hold "seven plus or minus two" information-bearing items. Atkinson and Shiffrin's estimate was developed from rigorous examination of a particular laboratory paradigm. Miller's was developed from an informal examination of reports of studies using many different paradigms. Which estimate should have priority?

Quite apart from a debate over the size of short term memory, the Atkinson and Shiffrin model is consistent with our phenomenological experience that things are either in our conscious awareness or are not. These researchers claimed that information cannot be operated on until an item is in short term memory, and conversely, that a piece of information cannot influence thought until it has reached short term memory. Experimental situations have been found that violate both of these assumptions.

Incoming information can influence the accessibility of information in long term memory, although the incoming information does not reach the level of consciousness. This point was illustrated in a series of studies using what is known as a *visual masking* paradigm. In this paradigm, a written word is displayed, and then immediately followed by a string of nonsense characters, for example, APPLE, followed within a few tens of milliseconds by the string &*^%$#@)*. Although the masked word is not perceived (i.e., it is *masked*) its semantic characteristics will influence decisions made immediately following presentation of the mask. For example, APPLE followed by a mask would be expected to speed the recognition of semantically related words, such as PIE, that are presented after the mask. This would be true even if the observer denied that APPLE had been presented. Analogous experiments have shown similar effects with spoken words.

Results like these indicate that stimuli are processed up to the level of semantic analysis although they have not been consciously perceived. In the terms of the Atkinson and Shiffrin model, information in the buffer must somehow contact long term memory without going through short term memory. However, it appears that this contact is quite limited.

It also appears that information can be placed in long term memory without going through short term memory. Under some circumstances, people can be shown information, fail to recall it in the short term, yet still retrieve it in another setting days or even weeks later. The related studies are discussed in chap. 6, Memory.

For further information about the Atkinson and Shiffrin model and about the studies that show the model needs to be modified, read Chapter 2/3Consciousness.

2.4 The Physical Basis of Memory

In addition to explaining immediate perception, a theory of consciousness must explain how we integrate information over time. At the end of the 19th century, William James (1890) distinguished between primary and secondary memory, loosely, memory for events over the past few seconds or minutes, and memory for events and information that may have been acquired hours, months, or years ago. The distinction has been carried forward into modern models of memory, including the Atkinson and Shiffrin (1968) model. Next, we examine its physical basis in more detail.

The brain is a system of approximately five billion electrically active elements, the neurons. Information about previous brain states can be held in the brain in two ways: by the influence of a past event on the brain's current pattern of electrical activity and by the connections between neurons themselves. These two types of information storage are believed to be the physical substrates of James' primary and secondary memory. Late 20th-century research in the neurosciences showed that repeated electrical activity can alter inter-neuron connectivity. This establishes the existence of a mechanism for the transfer of information from primary to secondary memory. It is reasonable to believe that early 21st-century research in the neurosciences will ultimately result in a detailed understanding how this mechanism works.

Behaviorally, the distinction between memory as neuroelectric activity and as inter-neuron connectivity can be inferred from several different types of observations. Experiments with animals have shown that electrical shocks to the brain will disrupt memory for events immediately before delivery of the shock without destroying memory for events in the distant past. Similar phenomena have been seen in patients who receive electric shock therapy for some types of mental illnesses. Surprisingly, this therapy often works, although no one is sure just why. The patients do not remember events immediately prior to receiving the shock, but remember temporally distant events. Animal studies have shown that certain drugs can improve the efficiency of transfer of information from the transient electrical stage to the permanent neural connectivity stage. Such findings suggest that someday it may be possible to develop therapies for debilitating diseases that are characterized by loss of memory, such as Alzheimer's dementia.

This discussion refers to the mechanisms by which memory works. Another way to look at the brain–memory relation is to ask where the major centers for memory storage are. It appears that memories, in regard to records of repeated patterns of activity, are stored widely throughout the cortex. What ties together different patterns so that we have a coherent picture of an event as it is going on and a retrievable memory that can be examined later?

The frontal and prefrontal regions of the cortex seem to be intimately involved in establishing coherent pictures of what is going on. This includes tying together the separate what and where information developed by the visual system and establishing coherent relations between sight, sound, and other senses. Suppose you are confronted by a barking dog. The association of sight and sound happens naturally. The apparent ease of the task masks a sophisticated computation. Although we know that these activities depend in some way on the frontal cortex, we do not yet know what these computations are.

There are three sources of evidence for the frontal cortex's involvement in tying things together over space and time. Brain-imaging studies show that the frontal and prefrontal cortex is active whenever a task requires integration of information over space or over brief periods of time. The frontal cortex is also active if a task requires active manipulation of information. For instance, suppose a person is asked to look at a word and also think of a semantically related term, such as looking at the printed word GOOD and thinking of BAD. The frontal cortex is more active in this task than it is when a person only looks at the word.

Studies of brain-injured individuals provide further clues about the role of the frontal cortex. Individuals with frontal-cortical injuries tend to show impulsive behavior and to have difficulty in developing a complicated train of thought over time. This suggests that one of the major roles of the frontal cortex is to inhibit irrelevant aspects of a situation from capturing attention, thus disrupting the development of a picture of events in context.

Finally, studies have been conducted in which macaque monkeys are required to identify an object, remember it for a brief period of time, and then identify the object when it is presented as a member of a pair of objects. The animal receives a food reward if it makes a correct identification. Normal monkeys can learn to do this quite well. Monkeys whose frontal cortex has been removed have great difficulty with the task. The explanation offered for this is that the normal monkey maintains attention on the memory trace of the first object, whereas the brain-injured monkey is unable to do this.

Memory storage, in the conventional sense of storage of information that can later be recalled consciously, requires a second structure, the *hippocampus*. This is a large neural structure in the medial temporal lobes, with projections throughout the cortex. The hippocampus appears to play a central role in tying together different parts of an experience, so that our record of a stimulus is attached to the context in which the stimulus occurred. This is what we normally mean by human memory; a person knows something if he or she can recall information relevant to a given context. This would be illustrated by answering questions like "What was the name of the man you introduced me to last night?" or, as is more likely in a psychology laboratory, "Recite the list of arbitrary noun–number pairings that you learned when you visited the laboratory yesterday." Neuropsychological studies have shown that removal of the hippocampal structures virtually eliminates a person's ability to answer such questions. In such cases, patients are said to have suffered *anterograde amnesia,* for they are unable to form memories for events experienced after the injury. Severe anterograde amnesia can also be produced by prolonged alcoholism (*Korsakoff's syndrome*), which has as one of its outcomes damage to structures closely linked to the hippocampus, although interestingly, often not the actual hippocampus.

At this point, it is worth recalling a previous observation. Most of the studies cited earlier involve either imaging of or intervention into brain processes. The outcomes are described in abstract information processing terms. It is not possible to make sense of the neuroscientific observations unless they are combined with a psychological model of human information processing and of ways to measure different aspects of that processing.

> *For more information on brain processes and structures related to memory, see* Chapter 2/4PhysicalBasisofMemory.

2.5 Behavioral Studies of Primary Memory in Humans

Discussions of the physiology and neuroanatomy of memory establish a link between brain processes, brain structures, and abstract information processing capabilities. However, they do not present a clear picture of the primary memory capacities of normal, healthy humans. That information is best obtained by laboratory studies. What we know most about is human memory for briefly presented verbal material, such as lists of nonsense syllables or arbitrary noun–number pairings.

Memory for such arbitrary verbal material is surprisingly short. Studies done as early as the 1950s demonstrated that a list of as few as three arbitrarily chosen nouns, such as DUCK, COW, and HEN can be forgotten within 30 seconds after presentation. The trick is to divert a person's attention from the material to be memorized, immediately after it has been presented. This can be done by having the person engage in a distracting task, such as counting backward from a large number by sevens. Experiments like this provided much of the motivation for the Atkinson and Shiffrin model, with its emphasis on the need to attend to information in short-term memory until there has been time to fixate it in long-term memory.

Suppose that conditions do allow a person to concentrate on information being held in short-term memory. What mechanisms are used to retrieve that information? The question is important because there are a number of situations in which a new piece of information can only be interpreted in light of information received earlier. This is particularly clear for language comprehension, which requires the continuous integration of information received over time. The word *he* in *When Harry woke up he saw the bird on the tree* has no meaning unless its referent, *Harry*, can be retrieved from memory when *he* is read.

In a series of experiments often considered classics of experimental design, Saul Sternberg (1969, 1975) showed that the time needed to retrieve information from primary memory increases linearly with the number of information bearing chunks currently in memory. It is tempting to conclude that this indicates that a person examines the chunks held in memory one at a time, in serial fashion. In the *Harry* example, a comprehender might count backward from *he* until a possible referent, *Harry*, is encountered three words earlier. It is unlikely that language comprehension is this simple. In fact, the finding that retrieval time increases linearly with the number of items in an arbitrary list, such as DUCK, HOWL, IRON, JUMP... ' Was HOWL in the list?' does not prove that list is being searched one item at a time. Nevertheless, the empirical finding is important, for it shows that the time required for retrieval and examination of information in short term memory varies in a regular way with the amount of information being processed. Alterations in the relationship have been used as a measure of efficiency of information processing. For instance, Sternberg's experimental paradigm has been used to show that certain drugs used to control epileptic seizures have the side effect of decreasing the speed of information retrieval from primary memory (MacLeod, Dekaban, & Hunt, 1978).

The distinction between serial and parallel searches for information in memory quickly leads to an involved discussion of how one would tell whether information is retrieved in a serial or a parallel fashion. This topic is discussed in chap. 2, Appendix A.

Although most studies of primary memory have involved memory for verbal material, there is a substantial body of literature on memory for visual-spatial material. Some of the most interesting studies involve manipulation of a visual image. The basic idea is that a visual stimulus (e.g., a picture of a letter) is presented and the observer is asked to make a visual transformation of it, such as turning it upside down "in the mind's eye." In general, the time required to make the mental transformation is a linear function of the time that would be required if the transformation were to be made in the external world. To get some flavor of the phenomena, suppose that a letter were presented and an observer was asked to imagine the letter as it would look when rotated through a fixed angle, θ, as in the following example:

FIG. 2.1. The time required to imagine the rotation increases linearly as the angle of rotation, θ increases.

Taken together, the studies of verbal and visual short term memory show that the amount of information that can be held in them is surprisingly small, and that the manipulation of information requires the mental analog of effort, for the time to complete a manipulation varies regularly and usually linearly with the complexity of the mental manipulation and the amount of information being manipulated. Further experiments showed that we are clearly dealing with two different memory systems, because providing that the individual efforts are not too attention-demanding, it is possible to manipulate verbal and visual-spatial information at the same time. (People can safely listen to the radio when driving a car, but accident rates do rise when drivers attempt the more difficult task of talking on a telephone and driving.) Alternately, a great deal of interference is observed if people attempt two verbal or two spatial-visual tasks at the same time.

There is general agreement amongst psychologists that one of the biggest constraints on human reasoning is our limited ability to hold information in primary memory. Nevertheless there has to be more to primary memory than the extremely small short term stores revealed by the laboratory experiments. For instance, in their experimental studies, Atkinson and Shiffrin (1968) estimated that primary (short term) memory can only hold two chunks of information at a time. The Peterson and Peterson studies showed that people can hold less than four items in primary memory in the face of interference. Yet, when people solve problems outside of the laboratory they display larger memories than this, and even larger memories than Miller's (1956) estimate of 7 ± 2. To illustrate, consider the following sentence:

> The witness, badly battered and bruised, was examined in a supportive manner by the lawyer.

The sentence cannot be understood until the last word has been read. (Suppose the last word was "physician." A different sort of examination would be implied.) But the word *lawyer* is 6 words from *examined*, and 14 from the start of the sentence. Examples like this make it clear that laboratory studies underestimate people's ability to keep track of multifaceted situations. On the other hand, the laboratory data is extremely reliable; the low estimates have been obtained in dozens, if not hundreds, of experiments in laboratories throughout the world.

Alan Baddeley (1986), an English psychologist who has done a great deal of basic and applied research, responded to the paradox by developing an expanded model of what primary memory is. This is often referred to as the working memory model, although strictly speaking, working memory is only one component of Baddeley's model.

Baddeley assumed that immediate memory, which he refers to as *working memory*, consists of three interconnected systems; two rehearsal buffers and a somewhat mysterious "central executive" process. (In some of Baddeley's research, the term *working memory* is reserved for the central executive. Here, I use working memory to refer to the entire system.) The rehearsal buffers provide a place to hold active representations of visual information (the "visual-spatial scratch pad") and auditory information (the "acoustic store" for sounds and the "echoic buffer" for rehearsal of speech information). In Baddeley's terms, Atkinson and Shiffrin were studying the echoic buffer, not the whole of primary memory. The rehearsal buffers are thought of as holders of information that is operated on by the programs of the central executive. In more recent writings, the central executive processes are more or less equated with attentional processes that fixate on an item in a rehearsal buffer, or perhaps create a transformation of it. This idea will be elaborated on in chap. 3, which discusses a particular class of mathematical models of thought known as *blackboard models*.

Baddeley's (1986) view of primary memory has been widely accepted, albeit in a somewhat modified form. In its original formulation, the central executive was left rather vague. This is a problem, because an information processing model cannot contain something equivalent to a *homunculus*, literally, a little man inside the model who takes care of everything that the model does not specify. If a psychological model contains a homunculus, then we must explain the psychology of the homunculus. On the other hand, the central features of Baddeley's model have been validated by subsequent research. This research showed that it is necessary to distinguish between the ability to keep in mind several things at once (e.g., driving and listening to the radio) and the ability to repeat, in rote fashion, arbitrary lists of numbers or words. The former ability would be a function executed by Baddeley's central executive, the latter by the echoic store.

The central executive is clearly the most important module in primary memory. Measures of central executive functioning have markedly higher correlations with the ability to do intellectual tasks, such as solving algebra word problems, than do measures of echoic store capacity (Klapp, Marshburn, & Lester, 1983; Engle et al., 1999). Baddeley (1986) observed that there are neuropsychological cases in which the patient's ability to repeat back a list of digits is virtually destroyed. In one case, the patient had a digit span of one. Such individuals can speak and comprehend sentences, a capacity that clearly requires the ability to record information over short periods of time.

As a result of these observations, many psychologists see the executive function of working memory as an attention and control device. As is explained in chapters 3 and 4, there are good reasons to believe that thinking can be thought of as activation of previously stored mental programs for processing information. You can think of words as signals for the associated program; seeing or hearing the word *dog* activates a program that retrieves what the perceiver knows about dogs (Miller & Johnson-Laird, 1976). The same could be said about the sight of a dog; the scene activates programs related to the scene. However, there is an element of confusion here because coherent thought requires that only relevant information be activated. If I were to be confronted by an angry dog, it would not be helpful to recall that dogs and humans are among the few species that can sneeze. What the executive function of working memory seems to do is to control the competition between potential thoughts so irrelevant ideas do not crowd out relevant ones during problem solving.

Viewed in this manner, the role of the central executive in Baddeley's computational model of the mind closely resembles the functions that neuroscientists have assigned to the frontal lobes. Currently, the situation is clearly incomplete. We know that a central executive function exists apart from the sort of rote memory evaluated by measures such as the digit span task. We also know where this function resides; in the frontal and prefrontal lobes of the brain. However, we have only a vague idea of the computations that the central executive performs to control attention. As we enter the 21st century, one of the most important goals of cognitive psychology is to provide a computationally adequate model of Baddeley's central executive function. This goal is inherently an information processing goal; we are looking for an algorithm as well as the place where the algorithm is executed.

> *For more information concerning human primary memory, read* Chapter 2/5PrimaryMemory. *Other relevant information can be found in the folders for chap. 3, a discussion of a particular approach related to Baddeley's ideas, chap. 5 (Memory), and chap. 6 (Visual-Spatial Representations).*

2.6 A Model of Consciousness

Having gone through an overview of information processing in the human mind, where are we with respect to consciousness? One way to summarize our knowledge is to outline a highly speculative model of consciousness.

Perception begins when light, sound, and perhaps touch and smell, transmitted from the distal stimulus, impinge on the sensory system and form the proximal stimulus. The proximal stimulus is broken down into features both within and across the different sensory modalities. We have a relatively good idea of how this breakdown takes place in the visual and auditory system. Our knowledge of the breakdown in other sensory systems is less detailed. The processed features are then reassembled in some manner, so that we perceive things such as barking dogs as coherent, external objects.

Phenomenologically, conscious awareness does not occur until the reassembly process is complete. Nevertheless, it is clear that a substantial amount of stimulus interpretation and identification occurs at a preconscious level. Recall the experiments that showed that the semantic characteristics of a word can be activated when the word itself is not consciously perceived. In addition, top-down instructions can alert the perceptual system to signal when an isolated target feature is present.

As a result, what arrives at the conscious level is a combination of signals developed both from bottom-up processes driven by the proximal stimulus, and signals from memory that have been activated by features of the proximal stimulus. Baddeley's central executive somehow managed to accentuate some of the features and suppress others, so that coherent perceptions are integrated over time; what we perceive now is selected features of the proximal stimulus interpreted in the context of the percepts developed in the immediate past. The importance of integration over time can be seen by reflecting on how easily we understand, *The speaker made a slip of the tongue,* and *The model put on her slip and dress,* although very different meanings are associated with *slip.*

What can we say about the neuroanatomy of consciousness? It seems unlikely that consciousness occurs in a single place in the brain. It is more likely that consciousness is produced by the totality of active neural firings all over the cortex. Somehow these are bound together. To refer to a previous example, on encountering a barking dog, a person's mind knows that certain shapes, colors, and sounds are to be associated with the same objects in the world. The individual sounds, shapes, and colors are detected by different areas of the brain. How are they bound together? We do not know. And we will not understand the mind–brain system until we find out.

For an expanded discussion of a model of consciousness, see Chapter 2/6Model.

3

Blackboard Models of Thought

3.1 Computer Programs as Simulations of Human Thought

Explanatory models in science are often based on metaphors to everyday experience. This chapter deals with *Blackboard Models,* models of human thought based on a computer programming technique called *production system programming.* The programming method is used to create problem-solving programs intended to simulate human reasoning. The method is also used in Artificial Intelligence, where the goal is to create a powerful problem solver rather than to mimic the successes and failures of human problem solving. Although blackboard modeling is one of the most common methods of writing computer simulations of human thought, it is not the only one. A second technique, *connectionist modeling,* is discussed in chap. 4.

The effort to build blackboard models is a specialization of more general contention that thinking can be understood by writing computer programs that mimic human reasoning. This is called the *simulation* of thought. Although the idea of writing simulations was proposed as early as the 17th century, serious efforts to create simulations had to wait for the development of the modern digital computer. Current efforts began in the 1950s, when Allen Newell and Herbert A. Simon developed the first simulation programs. A summary of their early work can be found in their book *Human Problem Solving* (Newell & Simon, 1972).

Newell and Simon argued that when people solve a problem, they construct symbolic representations of the external situation in their minds, solve the problem through internal manipulations of the mental symbolic structures, and then transfer the solution to the external world. This is what a computer program does, because a computer is a symbol-manipulating machine, not an arithmetic calculator. (Arithmetic calculation is a particular type of symbol manipulation.) Therefore, computer programs can be written to execute certain symbol manipulation rules. If these rules produce the same behavior as human behavior, then the program is a model of human thought. The comparison could go beyond a comparison of overt actions. The computer program could be examined to determine why it chose a particular action, such as making a certain move in chess. People could be asked why they took the actions they did, and the two records could be compared.

Of course, the comparison would reveal discrepancies between human and computer behavior. The computer program could then be rewritten, to bring it more in line with human reasoning. Further problem solving behavior could then be simulated, and the program corrected, until the program's behavior and human behavior were aligned. When this happened, the logic of the computer program would, presumably, be the same as the logic of human reasoning.

It is important to realize that the resulting theory is a theory of human thought at the algorithmic level, not the physical level. The physical computer on which the program is executed is merely a convenient device for exploring the implications of rules for symbol manipulation contained in the program. There is no claim that the mechanisms of the brain resemble computer circuits.

The simulation approach could lead to a proliferation of programs, each describing some aspect of human thought, ranging from playing chess to understanding text. If these programs had nothing to do with each other no general theory would result. However, it turned out that the same principles of programming, the *production system approach*, could be used to produce many simulation programs. Therefore, it was suggested that the logic embodied in this approach was incorporated in the architecture of the human mind. The suggestion is particularly attractive because production system programming maps nicely onto the architecture of human information processing, as discussed in chap. 2.

Production system programming begins with the *production*, a rule that can be interpreted as "when you see this pattern, take this action." An example in driving is "When you see a traffic stop sign, stop." In chess we have "If the result of making move X is that the opponent is checkmated, then make move X." More generally, productions are in the form P -> A, a shorthand for "pattern implies action." *Production systems* are sets of productions that collectively constitute a problem solving strategy. For instance, rudimentary rules for automobile driving would contain productions specifying what is to be done when one sees a red, green, or yellow traffic light. The action to be taken in the presence of yellow lights could be made conditional on the context, e.g., observation of police. Although this example is trivial, the idea has been applied to write programs for very complicated situations, including medical diagnosis.

The use of pattern -> action pairs implies that the patterns are somewhere. Computationally, descriptions of a situation are held in a data structure called the *blackboard*, hence the name *blackboard models*. A production is activated when its pattern appears on the blackboard. Its action may change the contents of the blackboard, letting one production communicate to another. To continue the traffic light example, one can imagine productions to the effect of "When a police vehicle is seen -> set the goal to be cautious," and "When the goal is to be cautious and a yellow light is seen -> stop."

There is an analogy between the computing structure of blackboard models and the primary memory–secondary memory architecture of human information processing that was outlined in chap. 2. This is one of the reasons that production system models are popular as simulations of human thought.

For an expansion on the idea of production system programming and its relation to human information processing, see Chapter 3/1ComputerSimulation.

3.2 Blackboard Models

Blackboard models of symbolic problem solving achieve their power by combining permanent production rules (in long term memory?) with a picture of what is going on at the time (in working memory?). The blackboard can contain information about the current state of a problem and the goals and context in which the problem is being attacked. To sketch one example, an algebra problem solver might contain the goal *Solve for the variable x* and the rules that follow:

> If the goal is to solve for variable x and the equation contains expressions containing x on both sides, set as a subgoal moving all expressions containing x to the left hand side of the equation.

The action part of this production does not directly do anything, but it does establish a context for the next production:

> If there is a goal or subgoal to move all expressions containing x to the left hand side of the equation, subtract all expressions containing x from the right hand side and add them to the left hand side.

The theme of production system rules like these is that problem solvers proceed by recognizing patterns as they occur in working memory. It is the first major generalization to emerge from the use of production systems to simulate human thought.

Newell and Simon (1972) generalized the ideas contained in simulation programs in another way. They described problem solving as a search through a network of problem solving states, where a state is equivalent to the knowledge the problem solver has at that time. The problem solver begins at the state described by an initial statement of a problem, and searches through the network for a state that satisfies the definition of a goal. Again using chess as an example, the initial state is the starting position, and the goal is to reach any position in which one's opponent is checkmated. Inference rules are used to move from one state of knowledge to another. In chess, the inference rules are the rules of piece movement; in geometry the rules are the rules of inference based on Euclid's axioms. The idea of searching through a network of states applies to chess, geometry, algebra and many other problem solving areas.

Newell and Simon then described a general purpose program, a *General Problem Solver* (GPS) designed to search through abstract state-spaces. They argued that the program was a model for humans, who are also general problem solvers. The GPS was successfully used to solve problems in a number of different areas, generally at the level of high school or college freshman mathematics and recreational mathematics puzzles. Although this level of problem solving is not considered highly intellectual, it does require more deductive reasoning than is typically illustrated in everyday activity. Other researchers wrote similar programs to solve problems of similar levels of difficulty. All in all, the GPS was an impressive effort. Therefore, the strengths and weaknesses of the GPS must be considered carefully.

GPS is a purely syntactical problem solver. Knowledge states are described as symbol structures and inference rules are described as transformations from one symbol structure to another. In a travel example, travelers might be described by their state of health, amount of wealth, and current location. An airplane flight would be described in terms of the required starting point, the change that it affected in the traveler's location, and the change it affected on current wealth. A goal could be described in terms of destination and desired wealth on arrival. (If I set a certain value on going from Seattle to Cleveland, then I must arrive in Cleveland with a tolerable decrement to my wealth.) Establishing the mapping between the program's internal symbol manipulating structures and the characteristics of the external problem is called *establishing a representation*. GPS only deals with problems after the representation has been established. That is, the program looks at changes in attribute 1, attribute 2, and so forth, with no knowledge of what these variables are supposed to mean. Newell and Simon (1972) argued that the same restrictions apply to the mind. In terms of chap. 2 (but not in the researchers' terms) they assumed that a "representation establishing module" establishes a problem's mental representation, and that a general purpose symbol manipulation module operates on it. GPS dealt only with symbol manipulation.

Opinions differ as to how close GPS is to an adequate theory of human problem solving. Simulation programs never exactly match records of human problem solving (*protocols*). The issue of how to quantify the match has never been resolved. In simulation studies, measures of human performance generally resemble measures of program performance more closely than would be expected by chance, but this is too weak a criterion. Demanding that the program and human responses match exactly is too strong a criterion. Scientific psychology needs, but does not now have, some way of evaluating simulations that is analogous to the use of goodness-of-fit measures that are routinely applied to statistical models of human performance.

Although the issue of comparison is an important one, it probably is not crucial. Conceptual objections were also raised. These are discussed in the next section.

The GPS, related simulation programs, and their implications for psychology are considered in detail in Chapter 3/2BlackboardSimulations.

3.3 Conceptual Issues

Conceptual objections have been raised both to GPS and to the whole approach of using computer programs as a metaphor for human thought. The most publicized objection is to the emphasis on symbolic computation. Two symbol structures are either identical or they are not; 2 + 7 is 2 + 7, not "almost 3 + 7" or"'like 2 + 6." It has been claimed that human reasoning is based on approximate matches (sometimes referred to as fuzzy reasoning) rather than the exact matching process envisaged in production system programming. A related objection has to do with the status of productions in long-term memory. In the Newell-Simon approach, productions are simply there waiting to be matched if their pattern appears on the blackboard. This makes long-term memory a static repository of information. It seems more reasonable, and certainly more consistent with what we know about human memory (discussed in detail in chap. 5) to think of long term memory as a dynamic system, where the availability of a piece of information varies over time, as a function of the time since the piece was used and whether or not related pieces of information have been used recently.

These objections are not fatal, for production system models have been proposed that incorporate the ideas of fuzzy pattern matching and dynamic changes in the accessibility of memory. The most prominent of these are the ACT series of production system models of thought produced by J. R. Anderson and his colleagues (Anderson, 1986, 1992), but there are others.

Production system models assume a process known as variable binding. Productions are usually defined in terms of manipulations of symbol structures containing free variables. To take an example from linguistics (where production systems are used, see chap. 7), a simple active to passive transformation can be written as: *Agent active—form-of-verb patient -> Patient passive—form-of- verb by agent*, as in *John loves Mary -> Mary is loved by John*, and *The man who shot Mr. Howard fears Frank James -> Frank James is feared by the man who shot Mr. Howard*.

Somehow, either *John* or *The man who shot Mr. Howard* is substituted into the *agent* position of the the production prior to symbol manipulation. But how does this happen in the mind–brain system? This is a deep problem. The blackboard model approach simply assumes it has been solved.

Blackboard models have to contain some device that ensures an orderly sequence of production activations. It is easy to imagine situations in which the patterns of several productions might match a data structure on the blackboard. To see this, return to the polysemous word *slip*. If the mind uses something similar to production systems to interpret words, how is the correct meaning assigned to *slip* and *cost* in *The slip at the ice-skating competition cost her dearly*, and *The slip at the boutique sale cost her dearly*?

A number of mechanisms have been proposed that can handle the problem of selective activation of productions. Some depend on the idea that productions vary in their availability over time; others involve selection of appropriate interpretations and inhibition of others. While the selective activation problem is not impossible to solve, it is not clear how it is best handled as a computer program concept. We certainly do not know how

BLACKBOARD MODELS OF THOUGHT 31

humans manage the equivalent of selective activation. Note that this conceptual problem is closely related to the general problem of maintaining coherent thought by inhibiting irrelevant responses. Assigning the problem to the prefrontal cortex, the executive program in working memory, or the control mechanism of a blackboard model tells us where the problem is being solved, in either an anatomical or theoretical sense. It does not tell us how the problem is being solved.

> *For further discussions of the conceptual problems introduced by blackboard models, see* Chapter 3/3Conceptual Issues.

3.4 Learning in Blackboard Models

People profit from experience. We can acquire new information that is then available to for use during problem solving, and we can develop new ways of doing things. Changes in behavior due to acquisition of information are traditionally called *memory*, while changes in ways of doing things are called *learning*. Although the line between the two is admittedly arbitrary, researchers who construct blackboard models have generally emphasized learning.

There is a huge literature describing how behaviors change as people learn to execute problem solving procedures—from recognizing classes of geometric designs to operating fairly complex devices. Learning takes place in two stages. During the initial stage, the learner seems to be figuring out what is to be done. This stage is characterized by slow performance and a relatively large number of errors. The learner tries out a number of hypotheses about what is to be done, and selects the one that minimizes or eliminates errors. In the second stage, the learner sharpens the perceptual, motor, and perhaps cognitive procedures required to execute the newly acquired procedure. This stage, which can be quite lengthy, is characterized by relatively error-free performance and a gradual increase in the speed of the response.

Not surprisingly, the greatest increases in speed occur early in practice, followed by progressively smaller increases as practice is extended. In many situations, response time has been found to be an inverse power function of the number of trials. If we let $T(n)$ be the time required to respond on the nth practice trial, the following equation applies:

$$T(n) = A + B(n+E)^{-\alpha}$$

where A, B, E, and α are constants incorporated to the data from a particular situation. This equation is sometimes referred to as the *power law of practice*. Rosenbloom and Newell (1986) pointed out that any theory of learning should reproduce the power law.

Newell's (1990) successor to GPS, the S O A R program (SOAR), contains a learning mechanism that does just this. SOAR learns when it encounters a situation that it cannot solve using any of its current productions. The program then retreats to a planning space, in which it tries to solve the problem with combinations of these productions. When a combination is found that works, the productions in the combination are tied together into a superproduction, or, in Newell's terms, a *chunk*. The program notes the conditions under which the chunk is to be used, then inserts the chunk into its repertoire of productions. The second time the program encounters the situation it can apply the chunk immediately, thus reducing the time required to solve the problem. The power law is reproduced by a progressive recombination of chunks.

J. R. Anderson (1990, 1993) has developed a series of simulations, widely referred to as ACT (with several versions over the years) that reproduce the power law and contain mechanisms that incorporate learning and memory phenomena. Learning is modeled by a process of chunk creation somewhat similar to the mechanisms in SOAR. The main difference is that two productions will be tied into a chunk if they are used repeatedly in sequence, without the intervention of a planning process. The power law of practice can be reproduced in this way. In addition, performance can be improved by the judicious use of memory. The ACT program stores nonprocedural information in a *semantic network* that links related pieces of information together. For instance, information about ROBINS would be linked to information about BIRDS IN GENERAL. (This notion is further developed in chapters 8 and 9, which deal with the organization of knowledge.) When a piece of information is used, those pieces linked to it are made available to the program. This is consistent with the findings of many experiments that have shown that retrieval of information from human memory is sensitive to the context in which the information is to be recalled. (This phenomenon is discussed in detail in chap. 5.)

Later versions of ACT contain a mechanism for learning by analogical reasoning. An ACT simulation of how people learn simple computer programming skills illustrates this. Suppose that the program has solved the problem of writing an algorithm involving repeated addition. When presented with the problem of writing an algorithm for repeated multiplica-

BLACKBOARD MODELS OF THOUGHT

tion the program retrieves the addition algorithm and alters it to handle multiplication. Human computer programmers do this all the time.

Both SOAR and the ACT simulations are impressive demonstrations of how blackboard models can be written to simulate learning. Whether the processes contained in the models simulate human learning is difficult to answer. At a gross level, the program behavior looks like human learning. However, the problem of measuring the correspondence between human performance and program performance, which was bad enough for problem solving programs, is exacerbated when we attempt to model changes in performance over time.

See Chapter 3/4Learning *for an expanded discussion of how learning has been incorporated into blackboard models of human problem solving.*

3.5 Higher Order Thought

The early production system models of problem solving emphasized step-by-step decisions, modeled by the action of individual productions. At each step, the decision to activate a particular production was made by analyzing the extent to which that production would advance the problem solver toward his or her goal. This was called a *means–end analysis,* and was thought to be characteristic of good thinkers.

Somewhat surprisingly, it was found that experts in fields ranging from physics to international relations showed a very different style of thinking. Instead of solving problems a step at a time experts appeared to categorize a problem as an example of a general class of problems, and then immediately apply multi-step solution methods associated with the class rather than the specific problem. For example, if a physicist classified a problem in mechanics as a balance-of-force problem, the physicist would immediately write down all force relations in the problem, without asking how knowledge of each of them would contribute to solving the problem. The description given here suggests that this method of problem solving is wasteful; it is not. Often the answer to a problem falls out from the application of previously acquired problem solving methods.

To explain this sort of behavior within the general blackboard model theorists have adopted the concept of a *schema*. (The term was actually introduced much earlier, by Bartlett [1932], to account for the way in which people recall meaningful material. This is discussed in chap. 5.) In modern parlance, a schema is an organized plan for solving a class of problems. The balance-of-force schema described above is a good example. A schema can be thought of as a sort of a superproduction, similar to a chunk in Newell's terminology. It contains a pattern part that states the conditions under which the schema is to be used, and a complicated action part, which specifies what information is to be acquired and how it is to be used. In some cases, schema refers to other schema. For instance, a balance of force schema might call on an addition schema to calculate the sum of forces bearing on an object.

It cannot be emphasized too strongly that schematic problem solving is very widespread. Indeed, much of what is taught in school mathematics can be thought of as the provision of schemas for problem solving, rather than a deep analysis of the concepts of mathematics. And the use of schema goes beyond problem solving. As Bartlett pointed out in his original work, schema can be used to organize recall of stories, by classifying the story as being of a certain type and then focusing attention on items of information that are important in that schema. To take a somewhat amusing example, people will recall different information about the description of a house if they approach it with schema associated with home-buying or burglary (Anderson & Pichert, 1978).

The concept of a schema fits well with the blackboard approach to modeling cognition. Schematic reasoning is driven by pattern recognition, as is production system programming. One of the problems with schematic reasoning, though, is that schema are highly situation specific. This suggests that psychology should move toward anthropology, by cataloging the schema people have in different situations. Although this may be necessary, it is still a step away from the goal of developing a general theory about how people solve complex problems.

Chapter 3/5Schema *contains an extended discussion of schematic reasoning.*

Chapter 3/6Summary *presents a summary of the ideas contained in this chapter.*

4

Connectionism

4.1 Introduction

In order to develop a theory of thought we have to understand the constraints that restrict our attention to certain classes of possible theories. The intuition behind blackboard modeling, and computer simulation more generally, is that only a few computing systems could possibly solve the complex problems that humans demonstrably solve. Therefore, the quickest way to understand human cognition is to understand what sort of computing the mind is able to do (Simon, 1981). This approach is called the *computer metaphor* for thought. The computer metaphor, which certainly has some validity, is the driving force behind the theory development efforts described in chap. 3.

An alternative approach, the *brain metaphor*, is based on the assumption that human thought is constrained by the type of brain that we have. The brain is a network of neurons, so any thought a person has must have resulted from a computation done by a neural network. Therefore thought can be understood by examining the computing capabilities of idealized neural networks (Rumelhart, 1988). This chapter examines an approach using the brain metaphor.

To develop the brain metaphor we have to have a language for talking about brain-like processes. This is necessary partly because of our limited knowledge about the brain, which forces psychologists to develop theories of the action of an idealized brain that is, inevitably, not an exact match to the real brain. However, knowledge is not the only limitation. Suppose that we knew how the brain is really connected. The mind could not grasp the implications of simultaneous activity in five billion neurons, with 5 billion × 5 billion connections between them. We need a language for talking about idealized brain systems because the actual ones are too detailed to comprehend.

Connectionism is a candidate for such a language. Connectionism, sometimes referred to as *parallel distributed processing* (PDP) is a collection of mathematical formalizations for describing computations in networks of idealized neurons. It includes provision for self adjustment of the networks to simulate learning.

For a further discussion of the logical and historical basis of connectionism, see Chapter 4/1 Introduction.

4.2 Computations in Neural Networks

The basic computing element in a connectionist network is the node. Psychologically, nodes correspond to mathematical idealizations of neurons. For this reason, connectionist models are sometimes referred to as *neural network* models, although the analogy is a bit strained.

Figure 4.1 is a diagram of node activity. Nodes can be thought of as being in a state of activation. This is represented mathematically by associating a real-numbered value with each node. Activation is then passed between nodes, by making the input to each node a weighted sum of the activation levels of all nodes connected to it. The weights are called the *connection weights*, and the weighted sum is called the *input* to a node. It is important to remember that weights can be positive or negative, allowing for the construction of neural networks in which activity in one node can either increase or decrease the value of the input to the receiving node.

After the input has been received, each node in the network calculates its new level of activation, utilizing an *activation function*. Several activation functions have been considered. The simplest is *threshold activation*, where the activation level of a node is one when its input exceeds a certain value, called the *threshold* of the node. In this case, the node is said to be active. Otherwise the activation level is zero and the node is inactive. In other cases node activation is computed by a *squashing function*, that maps the potentially unlimited value of the input into the zero–one interval. This allows the node to occupy a range of activated states. In some situations, activation levels are allowed to range over the interval –1 to +1, instead of the interval 0-1.

CONNECTIONISM

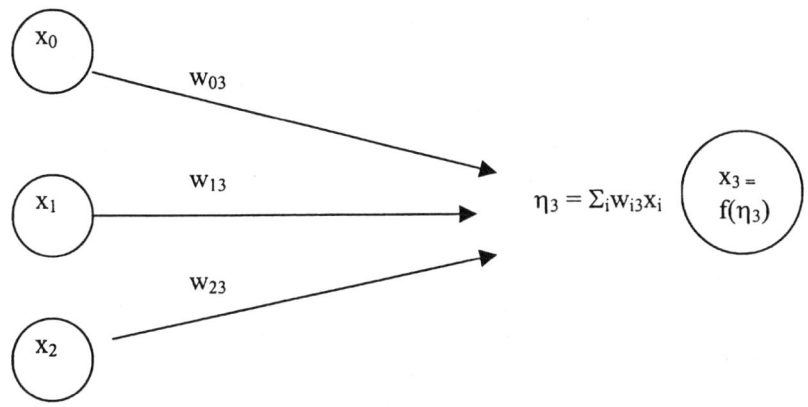

The justification for referring to connectionist models as "neural" or "brain" models is that the process of passing activation between nodes at least approximates the way in which neurons influence each other's activ-

FIG. 4.1. A connectionist (PDP) network is a collection of *nodes* and *arcs*, which are unidirectional links connecting nodes to one another. Each node has associated with it a current activation level, x. Arcs have weights, w, associated with them. The input to a node, η, is the sum of the activation levels of all nodes connected to the node in question (on the right side, above), weighted by the weights of the arcs between the nodes. The new activation level is a nondecreasing function, $f(\eta)$, of the input.

ity. If a node is considered a model of an individual neuron, a threshold activation function should be used. If a node is supposed to model the activity of a group of neurons connected in parallel to other groups, the squashing function is an appropriate model of group activity.

The connections between nodes determine the network's *architecture*. A problem is presented to a connectionist network by externally setting the activation levels of a selected set of nodes, called the *input nodes*. Activation is then passed between nodes until a stopping criterion is reached. At this point, the activation levels in a second selected set of nodes, the *output nodes*, define the network's response. Nodes that are not input or output nodes are called *hidden nodes*. Viewed this way, a connectionist model is a device for computing functions that map from vectors of activation levels in the input nodes to vectors of activation levels in the output nodes.

It can be proven that unrestricted connectionist devices are capable of computing any computable function (i.e., that connectionist models in general are equivalent to a universal Turing machine). Therefore, it is not interesting to say that a connectionist model could compute a particular function or be created to model a particular bit of human behavior. Such assertions become interesting when made about a connectionist model using a particular architecture. For instance, connectionist models without a layer of hidden nodes, in which the input layer is directly connected to the output layer, can only compute outputs that are linear functions of inputs. Therefore these models, sometimes called *perceptrons*, are not powerful enough to model human behavior. Our interest centers on connectionist models that have an architecture that might be related to the organization of the brain, and can compute functions that appear to mimic some aspect of human cognitive behavior.

Figure 4.2 shows three widely used architectures. The simplest is the *feed forward network* in which input units activate hidden units, which in turn activate output units. This network can be used to produce a number of stimulus–response patterns. For instance, a feed forward network can be used to produce the nonlinear mapping "Respond yes if stimulus A is present or stimulus B is present, but not if both are present." (The architectures that do this must have hidden layers.) Many studies have been conducted in which feed forward networks have mimicked human pattern recognition.

In *interactive networks* the nodes at one level feed activation back to the preceding level. Therefore, the processing of current input can be affected by the processing of prior input. This sort of network has been used to model top down effects in perception, such as the finding that letters are perceived more quickly when they are presented in a word than when they are presented in isolation.

In *recurrent networks* a feedback loop is established between nodes at the same level, usually the hidden level. Recurrent networks are capable of representing stimuli that are defined over time, because the present stimulus is 'interpreted' in the light of information about previous stimuli, as represented by information in the feedback loop. This means that the network can respond differentially to different temporal patterns of input. As an illustration, suppose that a connectionist model was constructed similar to Figure 4.2, with the input units representing written letters and the output nodes representing phonological features. In principal, such a network could learn to activate different phonological features for the sequence *ut*... (as in |utilize|) and *oth*... (as in |other|).

CONNECTIONISM

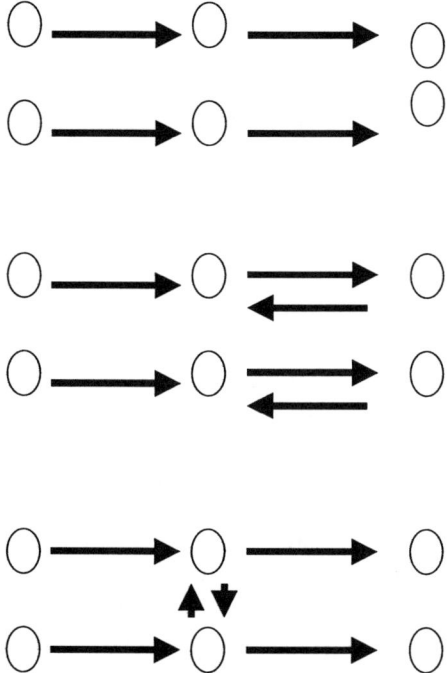

FIG. 4.2. Three types of PDP networks. Network (a) is a feed forward network, network (b) is a recurrent network, and network (c) is an interactive network.

These examples are intended to show pure cases of different architectures. In practice, a single network may contain feed forward, interactive, and recurrent links. Also, it is important to remember that activation may be positive or inhibitory. Interactive and recurrent links can be used to discourage, as well as to encourage, activity in selected regions of the network.

More details can be found in Chapter 4/2NetworkComputations. *The file includes mathematical definitions and illustrative examples of applications to psychological problems.*

4.3 Learning

Connectionist networks learn by adjusting the weights associated with the arcs between nodes, thus changing the extent to which the receiving node responds to activation in the sending node. This can be done in two modes, *supervised* and *unsupervised* learning. We consider the simpler supervised case first.

Supervised learning mimics the stimulus–response–reward sequence used in countless psychology experiments with both human and animal participants. A supervisor, external to the connectionist model itself, decides what the input–output mappings ought to be. Then an input vector is presented and the network computes the output vector, using its current weights. The output is compared to the output the supervisor desired. If the two agree, nothing is done. If they disagree, an error signal is computed. Its value is an increasing function of the discrepancy between the obtained and desired output. The current internode weights are then manipulated so that if the input were to be presented the new output would be closer to the desired output (i.e., have a lower error signal) than was obtained the first time. The process is repeated with other inputs, until eventually the system either stabilizes at some (hopefully) low value of the error signal, or produces a correct solution, in which all relevant inputs produce the desired outputs.

This procedure requires an algorithm for adjusting the weights. Three classes of algorithms have been used. *Error-correction algorithms* compare the obtained response to the desired one, and then adjust weights to move the two together. To take a simple example, suppose that there is a single output node, and its desired response is 1. In fact, the response is .6. The discrepancy is (1 - .6) = .4. The discrepancy is then shared between incoming connections in the following way. Call all nodes directly connected to the output node the *sending* nodes. If a sending node was active, and the connection from the sending to the output node had a positive weight, then that weight would be increased. If the connection was negative, then its absolute value would be decreased (i.e., the connection would be moved from a negative value toward zero). Next, suppose that the desired response was zero and the output node had the value .6. The discrepancy would now be (0 - .6) = - .6. The same procedure would be followed, except that this time the signs of the corrections would be reversed; connections with positive weights would have their weights moved toward zero, connections with negative weights would have their weights moved further away from zero, so that they were still negative but larger in absolute value.

The logic of these corrections can be seen by the following analogy. Suppose that a financier asked several brokers what stocks should be purchased and, after weighing the advice received, makes a purchase. Some of the stocks rise in value (good purchases) whereas others fall. When the financier next seeks advice, it makes sense to pay more attention to those brokers who gave good advice and less attention to those who gave bad advice. Error correction algorithms follow the same logic.

Two error correction algorithms have played a prominent part in the literature. The *generalized delta rule* is an algorithm for calculating adjustments to be made to the weights, in a situation exactly like the one just described. It can be shown that the generalized delta rule eventually produces a solution to any classification problem that can be solved by a connectionist network consisting of a single input and output layer. The rule is also of interest because its classification behavior is isomorphic to the Rescorla-Wagner model of classical conditioning, a widely used model of learning in biological systems. However, this approach is limited, because it amounts to learning by a perceptron and, as was noted earlier, perceptron networks can only learn classification rules that can be expressed as a linear combination of input values.

The *Back-propagation* algorithm generalizes the delta rule to deal with connections between input to hidden nodes. Varieties of back-propagation can be applied to interactive and recursive networks. Back-propagation is widely used in connectionist research. Although it is a useful device for finding good weights, it has no psychological or physiological justification. Therefore it is generally regarded as a way for finding weights when the purpose is to show that a particular connectionist network could solve an interesting problem, such as recognizing sight–sound correspondences in reading, but it is not considered a reasonable model of the learning process.

A third algorithm, the *Hebbian learning algorithm* (for the eminent Canadian psychologist, D. O. Hebb), is based on the assumption that in biological systems, synaptic connections between two neurons are strengthed whenever activity in the presynaptic neuron is followed by depolarization of the axon of the postsynaptic neuron, although the depolarization may have been due to the activity of a second postsynaptic neuron. In connectionist terms, the weight between two nodes should be incremented if both are simultaneously active. Because weight changes are not based on an error signal, this is not an error-correction algorithm.

One reason that the Hebbian algorithm is attractive is that physiological studies of learning have shown that something similar to Hebb's assumed learning process does occur in the central nervous system. A second reason is that the Hebbian algorithm can be used to produce networks capable of *unsupervised learning*. Networks using Hebb's rule can identify statistical regularities in the environment and use them to cluster objects into classes, without being told what the actual class memberships are. In addition, Hebb's rule can be used to construct network models capable of storing records of items, and then reconstructing an item when given part of its description. This resembles the reconstruction of a record, given partial information, that is characteristic of human memory (cf. chap. 5).

The generalized delta rule, back propagation, and the Hebbian algorithm produce networks that can adapt to their environment (i.e., learn useful classifications of input patterns) by adjusting weights between nodes. Two alternative approaches to adaptation have been taken. *Darwinian* algorithms begin with very large networks. The hidden nodes within these networks are capable of detecting more regularities in the environment than actually occur. The network adjusts to its environment by retaining input–hidden–output pathways that correspond to patterns that do occur, and eliminating unused pathways. *Genetic* algorithms solve the adaptation problem in the opposite way. The network begins with a fairly small number of classification paths. When two input–hidden–output pathways are found to be useful, in the sense that the environment regularly activates each of them, a new hidden node is created by combining randomly chosen connections from the hidden nodes in each of the original pathways.

See Chapter 4/3Learning *for an extended discussion of learning algorithms.*

4.4 Constraint Networks

Feed forward networks have a natural interpretation in terms of the stimulus–internal representation–output sequence familiar to psychologists. They also lend themselves to use as models of supervised learning. *Constraint networks* are a type of interactive network in which some of the weights on arcs between node are fixed ("clamped") at set values. A natural interpretation of such networks is to regard the level of activation in a node as representing a belief, and the weight of the arc between two notes as an indication of the compatibility between them. For instance, if we wished to represent political decision making we might let one node represent level of taxation, another represent voter satisfaction–dissatisfaction, and a third represent level of government services. The taxation node would be positively linked to the service node, and vice versa, but the voter node would be positively linked to the service node and negatively linked to the taxation node.

CONNECTIONISM 43

Suppose that a constraint network contains N nodes. The network can be thought of as moving through a space S defined by the values $\{s_i\}$ of the activation levels of the nodes. (In threshold networks, movement is confined to the 2^N positions defined by each node's being either active or inactive.) Transitions from state to state can be accomplished in one of two ways. *Boltzman machines* are networks of binary valued nodes, in which each state has a variable called the *energy* associated with it. The energy level can be thought of as a measure of the extent to which the constraints built into the network become satisfied. Somewhat paradoxically, energy varies from zero to minus infinity. Therefore, maximization of energy minimizes the absolute value of energy. This is sensible, because the energy function is defined in such a way that the larger the absolute value of the energy measure, the less the constraints are satisfied. Activation levels are changed until the network reaches what appears to be a state with the lowest possible absolute value of energy. The activation levels of the nodes are then interpreted as a solution to the problem. For example, in the political example outlined earlier, the final activation levels of voter satisfaction, tax level, and government service would depend on the values assigned to the weights representing compatibility and incompatibility of different beliefs.

A Boltzman machine can solve a problem by designating some states as assumptions and others as conclusions. The assumption states are fixed at one (active). Activation levels of the conclusion states are then varied until energy is maximized. To continue the political example, a mathematically inclined politician might fix voter satisfaction at 1 and use a Boltzman machine to determine what policies this implied. Hopefully, this simple (albeit implausible) example illustrates this idea. In practice, Boltzman machines have been used to solve much more complicated problems.

Constraint-based problem solving can also be displayed by *competitive interaction* networks. Network weights are fixed to represent constraints, and activation is cycled through the network in a manner similar to that used for feed forward networks. Activation levels are now permitted to have continuous values, usually within some restricted range. In theory, a network could enter into a never-ending progression of new states. However, this can happen only if activation levels are allowed to increase without limit. If activation levels are finite, or are restricted to fall within certain limits, then the network reaches a situation where entry into one state results in a change to another, then another, and finally back to the original state. Such behavior is termed *looping*, and the set of states in the loop is called an *attractor*. In the extreme, the loop contains just one state, in which case the network is said to have *stabilized*.

Unsupervised learning is defined for networks that stabilize. Suppose the input states are not allowed to vary. This is called *clamping*; the nodes whose activation levels are frozen are said to be clamped. Activation levels are changed by the normal method of passing activation from node to node until the system stabilizes. The weights between connections are then changed in such a way that if the input vector were to be presented again, the same stable state would be reached more quickly. A way of looking at this is to think of the network as being rewarded no matter what stable state it reaches.

Unsupervised learning can lead to the spontaneous formation of classes. If two or more input vectors lead the network to stabilize at the same attractor, then insofar as the network is concerned, they are equivalent. Mathematically, a class has been formed. To get a less nonmathematical point of view, imagine an apocryphal Martian, visiting Earth but not knowing anything about its inhabitants. If the Martian had a connectionist brain, the Martian could use unsupervised learning to notice that people come in two broad classes, men and women, defined by correlated features.

Chapter 4/4Constraints *explains the mathematical basis of Boltzman machines and illustrates the use of interactive, constraint-based problem solving to solve unsupervised learning problems.*

4.5 Illustrative Applications

This section describes a few examples of the application of connectionist models.

Some of the most important, controversial, PDP models deal with language phenomena. Language is considered a particularly difficult challenge for connectionism because connectionist networks develop rules for dealing with stimuli, such as forming the past tense of an English verb by adding *-ed* to the present tense, solely by detecting statistical regularities in language use. One of the central canons of the generative grammar approach is that language is not learned this way. The theories that have dominated linguistic research since the 1950s are based on the idea that children learn languages by selecting rules that are built into a species-general, universal grammar, and that fit the language environment into which the child is born (Pinker, 1993). One of the reasons linguists and psycholinguists hold this belief is that they believe the rules of grammar are so complex they could not be developed by a mechanism that only relied on statistical regularities. Such a device is called an *associationist* learner. PDP networks are clearly associationist learners. Therefore, if it can be shown that PDP networks can develop rules of the complexity found in human language, then one of the basic tenets of modern linguistic theory may need rethinking.

Precisely this sort of challenge to linguistic theory has been mounted. The TRACE PDP network recognizes phonemes in continuous speech. This is a challenging task, because there is no one:one mapping between the acoustic stimulus and the phoneme that is heard. (See the discussion of speech perception in chap. 2.) Connectionist network models have also been shown to be capable of "reading," in the sense of detecting letter string-sound correspondences. This task is challenging because reading includes the ability to pronounce words that follow regular rules, such as *save* and *rave*, and exception words containing the same substring with a different pronunciation, such as *have*. The widely accepted *dual route* model of reading assumes that people learn rules for the pronunciation of regular words and memorize exception words as special cases. The PDP networks used to simulate reading learn regular and exception words by the same associationist mechanisms.

Connectionist networks have been used to simulate learning of apparently rule-governed behavior. In one well known case that engendered considerable debate, connectionist networks were used to mimic human learning of the rules for forming the past tense in English, as in *jump -> jumped*. The same networks were able to learn exceptions, such as *go -> went*, and *hit -> hit*. Connectionist networks have also been used to detect structural rules that are defined over time, such as syntactical rules for forming Subject–Verb–Object (SVO) sentences. These rules include rules that discriminate between the types of nouns that can serve in the subject and object positions in a case sensitive grammar. For instance, a network that can detect structure in time can detect that words like CAT, MAN, and WOMAN refer to possible subjects of EAT and SEE, whereas CHEESE and MEAT can only appear in the object position.

Complex connectionist models are required to demonstrate linguistic phenomenon. The networks involved always include hidden units and generally contain both interactive and recurrent connections between nodes. Whether these demonstrations show that connectionist networks can learn language in the manner that people do is a matter of hot debate. The demonstrations show, with striking clarity, that Chomsky and the generative grammarians inspired by his work were a bit premature when they characterized associationist learning as "obviously" being an inadequate model of linguistic behavior.

Connectionist networks have also been used to simulate higher order reasoning. A common technique is to use constraint-based networks to show that a combination of known facts and principles, together with beliefs in their mutual compatability or incompatability, imply yet-unobserved facts. Many problem solving situations can be represented as problems in constraint satisfaction; a goal variable is maximized subject to maintaining certain other variables in reasonable bounds. For example, a traveler might wish to fly from Seattle to Cleveland by the shortest route possible, subject to the constraint that the flight arrive in normal working hours and that the ticket not cost more than $1,000. One can imagine a network that would deduce what flight to take by listing constraints, and then finding the flight that produced the minimum conflict between constraints. One of the interesting features of such a network would be that it would exhibit what we call "common-sense" reasoning. Suppose that a traveler did not wish to leave before 7 a.m. and did not want to pay more than $700. A production system would take the constraint literally, and reject a flight that left at 6:45 and cost $350 in favor of a flight that left at 7:01 and cost $695. A connectionist network could be constructed that would choose the 6:45 flight if it represented the least conflict between constraints.

This principle has been extended to simulate cases of problem solving that, historically, have been considered major feats of thought. In one case, Thagard (1989) used a constraint-based network to recreate Lavoiser's argument that the oxygenation theory of combustion provided a better explanation of the known facts about burning material than the phlogiston theory did.

For further details concerning these and other examples, see Chapter 4/5Examples.

4.6 The Variable Binding Problem

Chapter 3 presented the *variable binding problem*. To review briefly, when abstract rules are applied to concrete instances the free variables in the abstract symbol structure have to be bound to entities in the specific application. The problem is most easily seen in mathematics. The statement $x = exp(ln(x))$ is defined for any arithmetical expression whose value is a non-negative real number. Variable binding also occurs in everyday conversation. Take the English active–passive transformation, as in *Mary loves the cat -> The cat is loved by Mary*. This is an instantiation of the more general rule NP1 TRANSITIVE VERB NP2 -> NP2 IS TRANSITIVE VERB PERFECT FORM BY NP1 , where NP1 and NP2 are noun phrases that satisfy certain semantic constraints, such as the constraint that NP1 refer to an animate agent. The principle is the same in the mathematical and linguistic example. A previously established rule, a constraint network, is used as a template to create a new rule (network), in which concrete entities replace place holders in the original rule.

When psychological models are stated as production systems, variable binding is assumed to happen without explanation. Because connectionist theory is supposed to explain how the brain derives symbolic computing from subsymbolic computing the connectionist theorist has to explain variable binding rather than assume it. This has proven to be a difficult theoretical problem. Although connectionist models can handle variable binding by the device of copying networks, there is no known biological mechanism that might do the copying.

The term *binding* is sometimes used in a different sense, to explain how we see objects at locations, although the visual system analyzes object and location information at different places in the brain (cf. chap. 2). It has been suggested that binding, in the sense of gluing feature and location together, depends on the fact that when we look at an object, we simultaneously address location and feature information. This might establish a temporal synchrony between the neural circuits involved in analyzing the location and features of the same object. The temporal synchrony would provide a cue that the brain may use, in some yet unknown manner, to bind feature and location information into a perception of the distal object.

The perceptual process may provide a clue to the way that binding could be accomplished in PDP networks intended to simulate higher order cognition. In the example discussed earlier, if the goal was to perform a passive transformation, NP1 would be activated at the same time as *Mary*, in the original analysis of the sentence, and then nodes representing the occurrence of NP1 in the active and passive form would be activated synchronously, thus binding *Mary* to both of the abstract structures.

Whereas this line of approach is promising, we still have a long way to go to explain how the brain–mind system performs variable binding. Yet we perform it whenever we speak.

For further discussion of variable binding see Chapter 4/6Binding.

4.7 An Evaluation of Connectionism

Connectionism was originally offered to psychologists as a theory based on a brain metaphor, not a computer metaphor. In their most enthused moments, supporters of the PDP approach hoped that it might explain how the brain works, how the brain produces the mind, and at the same time, provide a way of designing artificial intelligence devices that could meet or exceed human capability. More progress seems to have been made toward the third goal than the first two. For instance, connectionist models are contained within mechanical speech recognition systems, but there is no accepted connectionist model of human speech perception. Connectionist modeling has certainly made a major impact on psychology, but it has not swept away earlier approaches. Just where does this theoretical approach stand?

There have been numerous and reasonably successful attempts to construct PDP models of behavior that can be tied directly to the brain. A popular target has been the simulation of speech disorders following brain injury by "lesions" (reductions of connections between selected groups of nodes) in networks capable of word naming. In quite a different effort, theorists have investigated the way in which connectionist networks for problem solving can be distorted by altering activation functions. Such work is motivated by a desire to understand how alterations in the brain's neurotransmitters might produce the disordered thought characteristic of schizophrenia.

Another way to demonstrate the power of connectionism is to show that connectionist networks are capable of the computations involved in high level thought, such as language and reasoning, that humans demonstrably do. Here, the connectionist (and for that matter, the production system) modeler has to walk a narrow line. On one hand, a model has to be shown to be sufficiently powerful to mimic human behavior. This is the sufficiency criterion described in earlier chapters. On the other hand, the model must not be so powerful that it exceeds human behavior. In particular, a model that amounts to a universal Turing machine could compute anything, and therefore, is not of interest to psychologists. Unrestricted use of connectionist networks, and unrestricted use of productions, both amount to tools for designing a universal Turing machine. Therefore we have to ask what restrictions on networks (or production systems) will bring the resulting models back into the realm of human behavior. This sort of investigation must proceed on a case-by-case basis.

How successful have such efforts been? One way to answer this question is to ask whether connectionist studies have changed our thinking about thought. They have. The "cognitive revolution" of the 1950–1960 period was based on the assumption that the attempt to explain higher order thought as an elaboration of simple learning mechanisms (*associationism*) was doomed to failure. Associationist models were thought to be insufficient to match the power of human reasoning. Connectionist studies have shown that this assumption is false. In general, associationist models are far more powerful, computationally, than they were believed to be. Therefore, when they are combined with reasonable architectural models of the brain they can provide illuminating insights into brain–mind relations. Alternately, it is possible to design a restricted connectionist model that fails to meet the sufficiency test.

There is one area that seems to pose a major challenge to connectionist reasoning. Connectionist devices can be looked on as devices that reason inductively by noticing correlations between features in the environment. People use contextual knowledge to change the inductions they make from identical statistical patterns of evidence. This is particularly true if the context in which a statistical pattern occurs influences explanations people give as to why the pattern might occur. Suppose that a person observes positive but imperfect correlations between features X, Y, and Z. If Y and Z are presented as possible causes of X ("colds and influenza both cause headaches"), a person is likely to accept the explanation that the presence of X indicates Y or Z, but that both are unlikely. This is a nonlinear rule. Or, if Y and Z are presented as possible symptoms of X, one may reason that the presence of X increases the probability of both Y and Z (a linear rule). Connectionist networks can be constructed to learn either rule, but it is difficult to see how a network could be constructed to switch from one rule to the other, depending on the context.

A consensus seems to be emerging concerning the possible uses of connectionist models. Such models do not necessarily sweep away those models where human thought is represented as symbol manipulation any more than quantum mechanics swept away Newtonian mechanics in physics. In physics, the choice of the appropriate model depends on the scale of the phenomena being studied. At the normal scale of human life, Newtonian mechanics is fine. When an object is very small, or moving very rapidly, the theory of relativity is appropriate. Symbol manipulation models are the appropriate choices to explain overt human reasoning as it occurs in activities ranging from playing chess to learning to solve algebra word problems. Connectionism may be a more appropriate approach for behaviors directly related to brain mechanisms, and possibly, for implicit learning and reasoning.

What connectionism may provide are models of how symbol manipulation works at the subsymbolic level. Such knowledge could then be used to restrict the class of symbolic models that we need to consider as explanations for human cognition. Unification of theories at the symbolic and subsymbolic levels is an important goal for cognitive psychology. It will not be easily achieved; there is precedent for a hard effort. Models at the quantum mechanical level are just beginning to give us an idea of why the Newtonian concept of gravitational attraction has to work the way it does.

An expanded discussion of the evaluation, with examples, can be found in Chapter 4/7Evaluation.

5

Memory

5.1 Overview of the Chapter

Thinking depends on memory, for if we had no memories learning would be impossible. Cognition would quite literally be reduced to knee-jerk reactions! We may complain about forgetting because we set such high standards for ourselves. Anderson (1990) used analytic techniques originally developed to evaluate information storage systems, such has libraries, to evaluate remembering. He concluded that human memory is an almost optimal solution to the problem of utilizing limited resources in order to retrieve the information we are likely to need, when we need it.

Any information retrieval system, including human memory, processes information in three stages. In the *encoding* stage information is abstracted and indexed for later retrieval. Encoding always represents a guess about how information is to be used, for the memorizer has no way of knowing the context in which a piece of information will be needed. In the second stage, *storage*, information has to be stored until it is needed. Storage has two aspects. The information itself must be maintained and its place in the indexing system must be protected. Whether or not information is ever physically lost from human memory is debatable, and perhaps unknowable. We clearly do suffer from distortions in indexing. To illustrate, I invite the reader to recall his or her telephone number, three jobs or houses ago. Finally, in the *retrieval stage* the system must respond to a request for information. Cues present in the request are used to construct a *retrieval path* that will lead through the indexing system to the needed information.

When memory fails it can be hard to determine the stage in which the failure occurred. Suppose you have the common, embarrassing experience of forgetting a person's name. Is this because you never attended to his or her name when you were introduced (encoding failure), because you have since met several other individuals who look like this person (storage failure due to changes in indexing), or because you cannot think, right at this moment, of any cues to suggest a name (retrieval failure)? Understanding memory is one of the major goals of cognitive psychology. The task demands and deserves rigorous analyses.

For further information and some examples of laboratory and naturalistic studies, see Chapter 5/1 Introduction.

5. 2 Ways of Studying Memory

One way to study memory is to observe how it influences our everyday life. Two classic examples of this approach are William James' reflective observations on his and others' memory, and Sigmund Freud's analysis of neuroses, which led him to conclude that behavior can be influenced by memories that are not expressed consciously. Folk wisdom leads us to believe that we know a good deal about memory. We are so sure of this that judges sometimes refuse to let psychologists testify about memory, on the grounds that the jurors know enough, from common knowledge, to let them assess the accuracy of eyewitness testimony. However this turns out to be a dangerous assumption. There are numerous, well documented cases in which witnesses gave convincing accounts of an event, but which turned out to be simply wrong. In other equally well-documented cases, the witnesses were right. Perhaps the only conclusion we can draw from these inconsistencies, and from the analysis of shrewd observers like James and Freud, is that naturalistic observations can suggest hypotheses about how memory might work, but controlled laboratory experiments are needed to develop scientific understanding of how memory does work.

Experimental studies of memory can be sorted into two classes, based on the extent to which the studies focus on memory, in the abstract, or on the interaction between memory and the meaning of the material to be memorized. Studies of memory in the abstract date from the mid-19th century investigations of the German academician, Herman Ebbinghaus. He invented the technique of studying memory by having people memorize arbitrary lists of nonsense syllables, such as the list KAK, WIR, TAM, JUP.

In the terms introduced in chap. 1, Ebbinghaus was interested in the study of memory at the information processing level, without concern for what the information represented in the external world, nor concern for the brain processes underlying mental action.

Ebbinghaus' research has stood the test of time. He was the first to notice the *serial position curve*, which relates ease of memorization of an item to its position on a list of items to be memorized. Items at the start and end of a list are remembered relatively easily. It is much harder to remember items in the middle of the list. Ebbinghaus also found that the accuracy of recall of arbitrary information first falls off rapidly, shortly after the information has been presented, and then declines very slowly for periods up to several months. This observation has also been verified many times. In fact, many modern studies of memory can be regarded as elaborations on Ebbinghaus' methodology and findings. However, there is another way to study memory.

During the 1920s, Frederick Bartlett, a professor at Cambridge University, conducted studies of memory for meaningful material, such as brief stories. Bartlett concluded that both the initial encoding and subsequent retrieval of memorized information depends on the person's having a *schema*, or a set of organizing principles, that reflect what information the memorizer already has about the topic of the material to be memorized. Subsequent studies showed that the same person can approach the same situation with two different schema, and that the schema used exerts a tremendous influence over what is remembered. If an art historian and a burglar take the same tour of a museum, they may carry away very different memories of items and locations. Why? Because they use different schema to incorporate their experiences into memory.

Experimental psychologists picked up Ebbinghaus' techniques almost as soon as he published them. This is partly because Ebbinghaus studied important phenomena and partly because it is easier to do carefully controlled, scientifically interpretable experiments with meaningless, than with meaningful, material. Measuring recall of the facts in a story as a function of the extent to which they conform to an established schema is not as straightforward as measuring recall of an arbitrary noun–number pair, as a function of the place in which it was presented in a list of such pairs. For almost a century after Ebbinghaus' published his work, the study of memory was very much the study of learning arbitrary relations.

Interest in Bartlett's approach revived in the 1970s. This was, at least in part, because people began to realize the importance of schematic reasoning in everyday situations. Some cognitive psychologists began to worry that we had concentrated on studying well-controlled situations at the expense of ignoring the normal mode of human memorization, building new knowledge into previously acquired knowledge. Although this concern is a legitimate one, it would be foolish to underestimate the very real problems associated with the study of "natural" memorization in uncontrolled situations. The modern literature contains a great deal about the importance of schematic reasoning, especially in education. Unfortunately, we cannot claim to have nearly as good an understanding of the role of schema in education as we do of the role list length and the number of repetitions during learning have on the recall of arbitrary material in an experimental situation.

A third way to study memory is to attempt to establish relations between brain mechanisms and the storage and recall of information. This is done by observing how brain states alter human memory and by extrapolating from studies on animals.

Until the 1980s most of our knowledge of the relation between brain states and memory performance was based on case studies of memory malfunction following brain injury. The most famous of these cases was patient H. M., who showed profound memory distortion following surgical removal of the hippocampus, a large structure in the medial temporal region of the brain. Prior to the operation, H. M. had been a healthy young man, working in a technical occupation. Following the operation he exhibited a profound anterograde amnesia (i.e., he had lost the ability to encode and retrieve new information). However, H. M. retained the ability to recall what he had known before the operation. These observations have since been repeated in a few other cases in which the hippocampus was damaged unintentionally. This work shows that there are two separate memory systems, one for storage and one for recall, and that the medial temporal region of the brain is an essential part of the storage function but not the retrieval function.

Research on brain-behavior relations in memory, and for that matter, in all aspects of cognition, took great strides forward during the 1980s, due to the development of *brain imaging* techniques. These techniques make it possible to look at brain structures without opening the skull, and locate changes in metabolic activity as a person is doing a task. In addition, advances in electrophysiology have greatly increased our ability to analyze electroencephalographic (EEG) records of the electrical activity of the brain. We have not yet reached the point that we have a real time "movie" of the brain, with spatial and temporal resolution of an actual cinema. However, the new techniques have already been, and will continue to be, stunningly informative about what is going on in the brain during memorization and recall.

Experiments on nonhuman animals have also yielded a great deal of information about neural processes underlying memory. This is due in no small part to our ability to perform invasive interventions with nonhuman

MEMORY

neural and physiological systems that would not be ethical to perform with humans. These interventions include the implanting of recording devices directly into the brain, experimentally controlled disruption of neural activity and, ultimately, sacrifice of the animal to conduct physical examinations of changes in the brain that can be associated with learning experiences.

When conclusions based on observations in nonhuman species are generalized to humans it is extremely important that we understand the theoretical basis of the generalization. For instance, the mechanisms of neuron-to-neuron connections appear to be the same throughout the animal kingdom. Therefore, when changes in synaptic connections associated with learning are observed in the sea slug (a mollusk), we have reason to believe they are the same as would be observed if we were to conduct similar experiments in humans. But let us take a more complicated case.

Histological studies of the brains of laboratory rats raised in enriched or standard conditions show there are more synaptic connections in the brains of the animals raised in the enriched environments. This finding has been presented as evidence for investing money in school programs that would (allegedly) provide school children with more interesting and challenging learning environments. Whether these programs would actually benefit children's education is an important question that can be answered by educational research. Extrapolating from rats raised in complex environments or laboratory cages to children in a special or standard classrom would require an impressive leap of the imagination.

More detailed descriptions of the different ways of studying memory can be found in Chapter 5/2Ways.

5.3 Ways Memory Systems Can Be Distinguished

A great deal has been said about different memory systems. In chap. 1, a system was defined to be a set of variables that maintain certain relationships between themselves. Recall also Plato's caution that systems should be defined in such a way that we carve nature at its joints. These ideas apply to study of memory. There are few, if any, laws of memory. There are laws governing the formation, retention, and retrieval of different types of memory.

Memories can be classified by the ways in which they are encoded and expressed. Obviously events are perceived using different perceptual channels, primarily vision and audition. The perceptual channels can be thought of as providing an internal audio or visual code for an external event. Different sensory codes can be manipulated in different ways, and are subject to their own distortions. To illustrate, consider the question "Why are the days longer in the summer than in the winter?" I answer this question by recalling a diagram of the Earth with its polar axis inclined with respect to the Earth–Sun line, rather than working out the argument verbally.

The notion of an internal code can be extended to distinguish between linguistically and nonlinguistic coded *verbal* and *visual* memories. It is also useful to describe memories in terms of their emotional content; evidence shows that strong emotions (especially fear) have an effect on encoding and retrieval functions. Of course, this is a matter of degree. It is hard to imagine a message or a memory that has no emotional content.

Classifications based on sensory and emotional coding tie memories to the physiological systems used to produce them. A second useful classification, between semantic and episodic information, is based more on logic than physiology. *Semantic memory* refers to memories for general principles about the way that the world works. *Episodic memory* refers to memories that are autobiographical, that refer to something the memorizer experienced at a particular time in their life. My recollection about the Earth's axis is an example of semantic memory. Recalling that I had pancakes for breakfast yesterday is an example of episodic memory.

Both semantic and episodic memory refer to memory for facts, about either the world or one's history. *Procedural information* refers to information about how to do things (e.g., riding a bicycle). Procedural information appears to act in a qualitatively different way than semantic or episodic information.

In addition to classifying memories by content, it is useful to classify them by the processing system involved. William James distinguished between primary and secondary memory. *Primary memory* refers to the objects and thoughts of which we are aware, or have attended to in the previous few seconds. Functionally, James' primary memory serves the functions assigned to the blackboard in blackboard models of cognition. The objects in primary memory can trigger further thoughts or act as a signal to take an action. *Secondary memory* refers to the (static) records we keep of things past. Information in secondary memory has to be placed in primary memory before it can be manipulated. To illustrate the difference, as I type this page my primary memory is involved in the development of my ideas, whereas my secondary memory is being used to supply primary memory with the word forms and examples that I use to construct those ideas.

Finally, memories can be classified by the extent to which they can be expressed. A person (or for that matter, an animal) must have a memory for an experience if it can be shown that having the experience exerts an influence over the memorizer's subsequent behavior. Many different behavioral tasks have been used to indicate the presence of a memory, and it is quite possible that different tasks tap different types of memories.

The simplest way to test a person's behavior is to ask them to recall the event in question, either by reporting it directly or by asking them to use information about the event to solve a problem. Memories that can be manipulated in this way are referred to as *declarative memories*. They are roughly equivalent to conscious memories. It is sometimes possible to show that the experience of an event has influenced behavior although the memorizer is not aware of the experience and is unable to make declarative use of the information in the event. Such events are called *implicit memories*. The distinction is important because it may be that different physical systems support the creation of declarative and implicit memories. To use one striking example, an anterograde amnesiac, who has lost the ability to form declarative memories can form implicit procedural memories. H. M., the famous patient whose hippocampus was removed, was taught mirror-image handwriting after his operation. The training took place over several weeks, during which time his performance improved. Therefore, he must have retained memories for motor procedures from one training session to the next although he had no conscious recollection of doing so. Although H. M.'s performance does not prove that declarative and implicit memories are physically different, it certainly suggests that they may be.

Table 5.1 presents a cross-classification of the various types of memory. It distinguishes between memories on the basis of their degree of expression (implicit vs. explicit) and by their temporal duration (primary or secondary system). The body of the table names some observable phenomena, such as priming, that are used to study each cell in the cross classification. We next look in detail at each of these phenomena.

TABLE 5.1

Cross-Classification of the Various Types of Memory

		Temporal Duration	
		Short-Term	Long-Term
Expression	Implicit	Priming, habituation, and sensization	Procedural learning, priming, and baseline activation
	Declarative	Studies of working memory and sensory memory	Episodic and semantic memory

For a further discussion and examples of the topics raised here, see Chapter 5/3MemorySystems/ClassifyingMemories.

Short Term Declarative Memory

In the cross classification, James' primary memory becomes *short term declarative memory*. This can be illustrated by the *digit span task*, which is a part of most intelligence tests. An examiner reads aloud a list of three to seven digits, randomly chosen digits, and an examinee repeats them, either in the original order or backwards.

In chap. 2, I describe Alan Baddeley's (1986) widely accepted functional analysis of short term declarative memory. Baddeley assumed that primary memory consists of two buffer systems, the echoic and visual buffer regions and a "central executive" system that controlled the manipulation of information in each of the buffer regions. Although just what the central executive does remains somewhat mysterious, we do know that its major role is the direction of attention, including suppression of information that is irrelevant to the task at hand. We also know where the central executive does its work. Imaging studies have shown that the prefrontal regions of the brain are active when a person is engaged in the manipulation of information in primary memory. These discoveries complement and extend earlier neuropsychological findings that people with brain injury in the frontal–prefrontal region become impulsive, have short attention spans, and have difficulty maintaining long trains of thought.

Baddeley's model fits well with the blackboard approach to cognition, as described in chap. 3. The blackboard acts as Baddeley's buffer regions, while the conflict resolution mechanism controls the flow of information into and out of the buffers. Failure of the conflict resolution mechanism results in too much information being placed on the blackboard in an incoherent manner, thus mimicking the behavioral effects of lesions in the frontal and prefrontal regions of the brain.

Short Term Implicit Memory

Short term implicit memories are exhibited by involuntary behaviors that occur shortly after an experience, that are not under the control of the memorizer, and that do not depend on the memorizer's being able to report the event. Sensitization and habituation provide two good examples. *Sensitization* occurs when a response to a stimulus is facilitated by one or more prior presentations that are not themselves perceived. The idea is best illustrated by an example. Suppose a word is flashed before an observer for the briefest possible interval that it can be exposed on a computer screen (about 35 milliseconds), followed by the exposure by a visual mask, a line of noninformative characters, such as !@#$%^. Most people will not recognize the word on the first or second presentation. Indeed, they may not be able to tell you whether a word was presented, for all that they are aware of is a flash. But if the same word is flashed several times in a row, the observer will eventually recognize it. The unperceived presentations have had an influence on the visual and memory system that makes the final presentation possible.

Habituation is, in a sense, the opposite of sensitization. Suppose that exactly the same stimulus is presented over and over again. On initial presentation, an observer (including nonhuman animals) will orient toward it. After a few presentations, however, the observer will cease to orient toward the stimulus, literally failing to notice it. (To take an extreme but commonplace example, airplane passengers will habituate to the sound of the engines.) However, at some level the stimulus is being noticed and recorded, because observers react when the stimulus goes away.

Sensitization and habituation are memory phenomenon, in that they depend on the past influencing the present but are usually considered to be changes in the state of the perceptual system. *Semantic priming*, as discussed in chap. 2, illustrates short term implicit memory within the (semantic) memory system. Recall the well-established fact that the presentation of a word will facilitate recognition of semantically related words. The oft-used example is the fact that people recognize the visually presented 'target' word NURSE more quickly if it is preceded by the 'priming word' DOCTOR than if it is preceded by BUTTER. Priming can be illustrated in situations similar to those used to illustrate sensitization; where the priming word (DOCTOR or BUTTER) is displayed so briefly that the observer is not aware, consciously, that it was there. Cross-modal priming can also be demonstrated. Auditory presentation of a word will facilitate reading of a related word. This shows that semantic priming depends upon the priming word's influence on the state of activation of information in long term memory, rather than its affecting the perceptual system.

For further discussion, see Chapter 5/3MemorySystems/ShortTermMemory.

Long Term Declarative Memory

In everyday parlance, the word *memory* usually refers to such things as remembering the name of a person met the previous week, recalling a newspaper editorial read the day before, or remembering a trip taken years ago.

Such actions require *long term declarative memory*. The memories are declarative because they are available for manipulation, and long term because more than a few seconds has elapsed between an experience and its retrieval. Long term declarative memory is usually displayed by verbal recall, but can be demonstrated in other ways. Declarative memory has been demonstrated in rats, by having the animals solve a problem in which they had to locate food in an unfamiliar situation by making an inference based on earlier experiences. There are a number of important distinctions between types of long term declarative information. These will now be examined.

The Episodic-Semantic Distinction

Long term declarative memories are *episodic* if the information retrieved is tied to a particular time and place. For example, when police ask a witness to identify a suspect, the police expect the witness to tie the person to the context of a particular event in the witness' own life, like the time the witness observed a bank robbery. By contrast, a memory is *semantic* if it refers to facts or beliefs not tied to a biographical context. To illustrate the distinction, I have a semantic memory that the American robins sing and have red breasts. I have in an episodic memory that I saw a particular robin singing in the woods just yesterday.

The episodic-semantic distinction is thought by many to be a psychological and a logical distinction. The reason is because episodic and semantic memories respond differently to various manipulations. One of these differences is the effect of retroactive interference on these two types of memory. *Retroactive interference* occurs when one loses the ability to recall an experience because other related experiences have occurred during the retention interval. Retroactive interference exerts a strong influence on retrieval of episodic information but has little, if any, effect on the retrieval of semantic information. Returning to the robin example, if I were to have seen a number of other birds, including other robins, in the 24 hours after I saw the robin in the woods, the first robin might have been forgotten or confused with the others. However, I could learn a number of new facts about robins (they migrate, they have brown backs) without much risk to my ability to recall that robins have red breasts. Indeed, in some circumstances, finding out new facts will cause me to organize new and old facts in a new way, so that recall of the original fact may actually be improved.

Although such evidence can be interpreted as arguments for a psychological distinction between semantic and episodic memory, the case for two memory systems is not airtight. It could be that it is simply easier to retrieve semantic than episodic memory because episodic retrieval requires that a piece of information be tied to the context of its acquisition, whereas semantic retrieval is context free. In fact, semantic information may be acquired by repetition of the same material in different contexts. When school children learn the addition table, each rehearsal is an episodic event, but is also an overlearning trial in Ebbinghaus's sense, insofar as the mathematical relations are concerned. Because the (highly similar) episodic events interfere with each other when the semantic relations are being overlearned, the student will eventually learn that $7 + 2 = 9$, but may not know when or where this fact was first learned.

A second argument for the reality of the semantic-episodic distinction is based on neuropsychological case reports. Episodic recall may be disrupted by injuries to the brain, such as concussions. These can cause a retrograde amnesia that extends backward in time. Memory for events is worst for events that occurred immediately before the injury, and is better for events that occurred some time prior to the injury. Semantic information is generally much more robust. Although lost identity themes are popular in the movies, cases of lost identity due to brain injury are rare. Cases of confusion about the present and recent past situations are common. When a person is revived after losing consciousness "Where am I?" is a much more likely question than "Who am I?"

As we have noted, damage to the medial temporal regions of the brain may also produce anterograde amnesia, in which the individual loses the ability to form new episodic memories. It is unclear whether an anterograde amnesiac also loses the ability to form new semantic memories.

The Dual Coding Hypothesis

The *dual coding hypothesis* is the conjecture that there are separate memory systems for visual and verbal material. The hypothesis is in accord with our subjective experience, for we certainly can recall verbal descriptions and visual experiences. Research on intelligence has shown that individual differences in the ability to reason about visual and verbal material are almost independent of each other, especially at high levels of ability (Carroll, 1993; Hunt, 1995). This has lead to the speculation that people have either visual or verbal styles of learning. In the extreme, some people have claimed that education should be adjusted to accommodate individual students' preferences for visual or verbal representations of information.

A somewhat different speculation is that there are two systems of memory, and that information management can be improved by using one system to help the other. One observation that lead to this conclusion is that it is easier to recall a list of nouns that name imageable things, such as DOG, BUILDING, SHIP, than it is to recall a list of abstract nouns, such as

WARMTH, FRIENDS, HISTORY. The conscious use of imagery to improve recall is an important part of techniques for improving memory. The most famous of this is the *method of loci*, a technique attributed to classic Greek and Roman orators. The memorizer recalls some well known locality and imagines walking around it and placing each item to be remembered in a familiar location. When the list is to be recalled, the memorizer takes another imagined walk around the location and picks up the items, all in the mind's eye.

Although the dual coding hypothesis accords with our subjective experience, it cannot be evaluated by behavioral observations. The reason for this has to do with the three-stage nature of memory. No one questions the fact that we can perceive visual and verbal stimuli, so visual and verbal information are clearly separate in primary memory. Similarly, at the recall stage, we are capable of recreating visual or verbal primary memory representations from information in long term memory. We can, for instance, recall the name of the person whose face is on a one dollar bill, or we can recall what a dollar bill looks like. But have we recalled the name and the picture from separate locations in long term memory, or has the mind–brain retrieved the same record in each case and executed different computations on that record to produce either a visual or a verbal representation? An observer outside of the brain–mind system cannot discriminate between these alternatives.

But what about an "inside observer," a neuroscientist who could look directly at the brain as people tried to retrieve visual or verbal memories? The dual coding hypothesis would be verified if neuroscientists could locate separate areas of the brain whose behavior meets two criteria. The first is that the areas should be separately active when verbal or visual information is retrieved from long term memory. The second is that areas that are active during retrieval from long term memory must be in addition to areas that are active when people do visual or verbal tasks that do not depend on long term memory retrieval. Another way to say this is that the imaging studies must differentiate between areas that are active in visual and verbal short term memory tasks (which have been identified), and areas that are active during tasks requiring long term memory. Active searches for areas that fulfill these criteria are currently being conducted.

It is worth pointing out that the usefulness of various learning tricks (or mnemonic techniques) involving imagery does not depend on the dual coding hypothesis being true or false. These techniques either work or they do not, on the basis of behavioral evidence. There is also a good cognitive neuroscience argument for them. The existence of separate primary memory regions for verbal and visual codes is well established. Coordination between these areas could improve the encoding and retrieval stages of memory, even if information is held in a universal code during the retention interval.

Emotional Memories

All experiences elicit some emotion, but the amount and type of emotion elicited varies widely. Studies of nonhuman animals have shown that highly emotional experiences (usually involving fear) activate the amygdala, a brain structure close to the hippocampus. This has the effect of facilitating learning. For example, under some circumstances a single electric shock following a movement can produce permanent suppression of a motor response. The data on human memory, where the emotional arousal is far less intense, presents a more mixed picture. Emotional arousal sometimes helps and sometimes hurts our ability to remember an experience. This phenomenon has been summarized in the *Yerkes-Dodson law*, which stated that emotional arousal assists learning and memory up to a point of optimum activation, and then hurts learning if it is increased beyond that point. Unfortunately, though, this qualitative observation does not tell us what the proper degree of emotion is in a particular situation.

The *Easterbrook hypothesis* (Easterbrook, 1959) amplifies on the Yerkes-Dodson law in a helpful way. Easterbrook argued (and subsequent research has verified) that the effect of emotional arousal is to focus attention on those aspects of an experience that are associated with the relevant emotion. The result is an increase in the retention of some aspects of an experience with a concomitant drop in retention of others. A study by Loftus and Byrne (1982) provides an excellent example. They asked university students to view slides of an initially innocent scene of people in a parking lot outside of a bank. The slide show then switched to a bank robber, who ran into the parking lot and shot a small child. The scenes of the child being shot were especially graphic. This had an amnesic effect. Compared to a control group, people who saw the bank robber scene tended to forget ancillary information, such as license plate numbers, that had been presented immediately prior to the shooting scene. In theoretical terms, it is reasonable to say that focusing attention on the emotion-grabbing aspects of the experience interfered with encoding information about nonemotional aspects.

The Easterbrook (1959) hypothesis applies to the encoding state. Emotions are part of the context of a situation, and as such, may become cues for memory. For instance, it has been shown that information acquired when a person is in a happy or sad mood may be better recalled if the mood at retrieval time matches the mood at encoding time. Note, though, that this effect refers to a temporary mood state. People in chronic states of depression generally show poor memories. Although this could be partly due to the physiological effects associated with depression, at least some of the memory effects appear to be due to a generalized apathy. Most encoding strategies require effort. For example, one of the recommended strategies for remembering name–face associations is to repeat a person's name while looking at them. The method of loci described above requires the conscious execution of a somewhat unusual memorizing strategy. Depressed individuals, almost by definition, do not make these efforts. Therefore, their retention facilities could be normal, whereas their encoding and retrieval strategies are deficient. The result is poor performance on declarative memory tasks.

Finally, the physiological effects of emotional stress may influence memory consolidation at the biological level. There are a number of drugs that block consolidation of information from primary into long term memory. We also know that emotional stress alters neurotransmission, because the effects of stress can be countered by other drugs. It could be that the biochemical effects of stress mimic those of some amnesic drugs. However, we will not have a complete picture of the biological effects of stress upon memory until we have a clear picture of the physiology of normal memory consolidation. And understanding that process would be a huge step forward in cognitive neuroscience.

For amplification, see Chapter 5/3MemorySystems/ExplicitLongTermMemory.

Implicit Long Term Memory

Implicit long term memory for an event is demonstrated when it can be shown that the experience of the event influences subsequent behavior, exhibited well after the event, although the event itself cannot be retrieved as a cognitive object, as in recall and recognition experiments. The term *implicit memory* has been used for two different sorts of information retrievals. I use the term *heightened activation* to refer to a situation in which a person has an experience that subsequently is shown to have altered the semantic and/or emotional response that the person makes to certain stimuli, although the individual does not have any declarative memory of the experience. *Procedural memory* refers to a demonstration that a person knows how to do something, without declarative memory of the procedure or when it was acquired. A common example is riding a bicycle, although many more cognitive examples can be found.

Memories associated with events prior to electroconvusive shock (ECS) therapy provide a dramatic illustration of heightened activation. ECS is sometimes used to ameliorate the severity of psychotic episodes. Although the mechanism is not clear, the treatment often works. Patients receiving ECS do not have declarative memory of the treatment or of events immediately prior to it. However, they may display emotional discomfort when returned to the room where the therapy was given.

Heightened activation can be shown in situations that are much less dramatic than ECS therapy. In studies using the *word completion paradigm*, a participant is shown a list of words containing either the word MOTOR or MOTEL. (Of course, the effect can be shown with other words.) Suppose further that at some later time the person is unable to recall the words on the list (i.e., declarative memory fails). The person is then shown word stems and asked to complete them. There will be a heightened tendency to complete MOT__ with MOTOR if MOTOR was on the original (and unrecalled) list, or with MOTEL if MOTEL was on the original list. The tendency fades over a period of several hours. What is interesting is that this tendency appears to be independent of the ability to recall the original list. Perhaps the most impressive demonstration of this sort is that anterograde amnesiacs, who have virtually no declarative memory for the word list, will nevertheless use words on the list to complete the word stems. Furthermore, the tendency fades in amnesiac patients in a way almost identical to the way that it fades in normal participants.

The *process dissociation* procedure is an amplification of the word completion paradigm that can be used to demonstrate implicit memory in normal individuals. The procedure is as described earlier, except that the participant is told to complete the word stems without using any of the words on the original list. Nevertheless, in some circumstances, people will show an increased tendency to use the words that they would not use if they had declarative memory of them.

It is not clear whether implicit heightened activation and overt declarative memory are the products of two different systems, or whether implicit memory may succeed where declarative memory fails because declarative memory makes higher demands on the retrieval system than does implicit memory. In the ECS case, for instance, it may be that recognition of a few cues about an experience is sufficient to reinstate an emotional response, whereas more cues are required to reinstate a declarative memory. If ECS disrupts the encoding process, as seems likely, the patient might have consolidated enough information to trigger an emotion but not enough to trigger recall. Therefore, if one wants to argue for separate implicit and explicit memory systems, it is necessary to prove that different variables affect performance on implicit and explicit memory tasks. There is some current research that can be interpreted this way.

In contrast to heighted activation, procedural memory definitely does seem to follow different laws of memory than those that apply to declarative learning. One of the most striking observations is that procedural skills can be taught to anterograde amnesics, who by definition are unable to acquire declarative information. The famous patient HM was taught how to do mirror-image writing, even though he did not recall the training sessions.

The evidence just described only touches on the findings that have been cited to support the contention that there are separate systems supporting explicit and implicit memory. The behavioral evidence is not clear cut. Everything we know is consistent with the hypothesis that there are two memory systems, but it might be that the tasks used to illustrate declarative memory may simply make higher demands on retrieval than do the tasks used to illustrate implicit recall. If this is the case, successful functioning of the declarative system should be statistically dependent on successful functioning of the implicit system. There is some evidence that this is not the case. Instead, success on some declarative tasks seems to be statistically independent of success on implicit memory tasks, suggesting that the two really are separate systems. (See the discussion of *process dissociation* in the main text.) Alternately, it might be that the retrieval demands of implicit and declarative tasks are different, and that whether they can be met depends on how the information was initially encoded. This raises a definitional issue: When someone claims that implicit and declarative memories are different systems, is this a claim that there are two completely separate memory processes, or that implicit and declarative memory differ only in the encoding, retrieval, or retention phases?

Because of these ambiguities in theory, I do not believe that the dispute over whether implicit and declarative memory are disjunct systems is likely to be settled by behavioral studies. Instead, psychologists will explore specific one- and two-system models, to see which accounts best for the data from a variety of paradigms contrasting implicit and declarative memory.

It is conceivable that at some point, brain imaging studies will show that there are regions of the brain that are active during implicit but not declarative memory tasks, and other regions that are active in declarative but not implicit tasks. Such a finding would be definitive evidence for the existence of two systems of memory. Failure to find different regions of activity would not be definitive evidence against a two-system model because the two systems could be so closely intertwined in the brain that we could not discriminate them.

Freudian Repression and Recovered Memories

The activation of implicit memories could be thought of as "unconscious cognition." If so, the experimental demonstrations suggest that unconscious reasoning is quite primitive. It seems to be limited to a vague tendency to recognize that something has occurred before, and perhaps that that something had an emotional connotation. More complicated reasoning seems to require declarative memory.

Sigmund Freud, the founder of psychoanalysis, held a very different view. Freud believed that quite complicated reasoning, including sexual and aggressive fantasies, occurred at the unconscious level. He believed that the emotional implications of such memories were examined by some sort of censor, and that the memories became repressed if they were too harmful to a person's self-concept. However, the act of repression was seldom complete; repressed memories appeared in unwanted and distorted representations, such as obsessive or irrational behaviors. The goal of psychoanalysis was to uncover the repressed memories and assist the patient in understanding them. Freud hoped that then the unwanted behaviors would disappear. Freud had a very different picture of implicit memory than that presented by modern cognitive psychologists, who believe that unconscious reasoning is limited to a general activation of associates in an inadequately encoded memory, rather than due to repression of a fully developed thought.

The debate over the nature of implicit memory has resurfaced in an unusual arena, the courtroom. In the typical case, the complaining person alleges that he or she has suffered a serious harm, such as sexual abuse, in the distant past. In most cases, adults claim that the incident took place during their childhood, as much as 20 years before. The complaining person further alleges the memory was repressed, and that they were only consciously aware of it after the repression had been removed through psychotherapy. The complainant then seeks some sort of redress from the person who committed the abuse. Although the resulting testimony can be dramatic, scientists who study memory are concerned about its accuracy.

Cognitive psychologists do not deny that an event can be forgotten for a long period of time, and then be retrieved when appropriate cues are presented. What they question is the mechanism of repression. A further point of concern is that the event alleged to have happened would have been a highly emotional one, and that, as was reported above, emotional events are the sort of events a person is most likely to remember.

Why, then, would a person appear to have suddenly recalled an event that they had never reported before? There are two possibilities. One, which always has to be considered when damage lawsuits are involved, is that the complaining person is simply lying. A less heinous explanation is also possible.

Memory is a reconstructive act, in which people do not clearly distinguish between information that was encoded at the time of the event to be recalled and information about the event that was received at some later time. Therefore, if a person learns, after the fact, that it was reasonable to assume that the to-be-remembered event had certain characteristics, then the event is likely to be recalled as having them. Such confusions are surprisingly easy to demonstrate. The literature abounds with reports of situations where experimenters induce students to report things that simply did not happen. The example that most captures my own imagination was a study in which college students were induced to recall having met Bugs Bunny during a childhood visit to Disneyland. It is very doubtful that such a meeting occurred, as the Bugs Bunny character is owned by Warner Brothers, not the Disney Corporation (Braun, Ellis, and Loftus, in press).

Do repressed, then recovered, memories exist? Cognitive psychologists who question the repression and recovery mechanisms point out that the clinical and legal reports seldom, if ever, have independent corroboration, and cite experiments such as the Bugs Bunny study just described to show that apparently repressed memories could be produced by post-event suggestions. Clinical psychologists who believe in repression see the repressed memory phenomenon as fitting into their theories about memory. They dismiss the experimental studies because the experiences to be recalled do not involve emotional trauma. Because it would be unethical to induce an emotional trauma experimentally, it is hard to see how this dispute can be resolved by scientific means.

For further discussion of the implicit–explicit distinction, see Chapter 5/3MemorySystems/ImplicitLongTermMemory.

This review barely touches on the voluminous literature on the existence and nature of different types of memory. The reader is urged to examine the more detailed discussions in Chapter 5/3MemorySystems.

5.4 A Model of Memory

The huge literature on memory can be summarized by a few experimental principles. Taken together, these principles constitute a theoretical model. It is certainly not my intention to construct a new theory of memory. The ideas to be presented are freely borrowed from the writings of numerous investigators.

The first set of principles deal with encoding. In chap. 2, I argued that we should think of information about the environment as being presented along parallel perceptual channels. Information enters the channels prior to conscious perception, and is then routed both to the buffer sections of working memory (collectively, the blackboard in blackboard models), and to long term memory. When the perceptual information reaches long term memory it will increase the activation level of related engrams. If activation is sufficient, information from the engrams will also be presented to the working memory area. At this point, there might be a switch in channels. For instance, when we see a familiar person, the visual percept will arouse the memory for their name.

Often, such arousals will be involuntary. In *Stroop experiments* observers are shown words written in colored ink, and asked to name the color of the ink. It is quite difficult to respond to a color name written in ink of a different color, as in the word RED printed in green ink. The explanation offered here is that the form of a word is so associated with its name that the form name is aroused involuntarily, prior to entry of the percept into working memory.

In order to create a unified percept observers have to combine information from different perceptual channels. Object perception is a good example of this process. We perceive objects as a form and a color at a location, although the brain processes form and color along the ventral visual stream (channel) and location information along the dorsal stream. When we combine features to perceive an object, we often do a considerable trimming of data, for we selectively attend to different parts of the perceptual field. This includes selective attention to information received from long term memory. Here, we look to language perception for an example. When we read the sentence, *The spy found a bug in his apartment,* the insect meaning of bug is suppressed within a few tens of milliseconds after having been read. Both perception and language comprehension would be impossible if such suppression did not happen. The mind would be so busy exploring potential, but unlikely, interpretations of the proximal stimulus that we could not meet the real time demands of comprehension.

The extensive coordination required to form a percept implies that there is an attention and coordination center somewhere in the brain–mind system. In fact, we know where: in the frontal and prefrontal regions of the forebrain. This center is essential to the formulation of a percept that is tied to a temporal context, because retaining information in working memory (on the blackboard, in theoretical terms) depends on the suppression of incoming irrelevant, but potentially interfering, information. It is worth noting that primates, and especially humans, appear to be much better at doing this than are nonprimate species. This is not surprising. The frontal lobes occupy a higher proportion of the volume of the brain in primates than in nonprimates.

Emotionality appears to affect memorization in two ways. First, if strong emotions are associated with any subset of the cues present in the proximal stimulus, then attention will be focused on those cues. This makes the emotion-inducing cues likely candidates for incorporation into the engram, and reduces the possibility that nonemotional cues will also be incorporated. Second, an aroused emotion is part of the cue in the proximal stimulus, and therefore, is a candidate for incorporation into the engram.

For a unified percept to be stored there has to be some center that can present the unified percept to long term memory, so that encoding can occur. The hippocampus and related medial temporal lobe structures seem to serve this function. It is worth noting that if a coordinating center were not present it would be difficult, if not impossible, to store a record of a stimulus associated with a particular context. Instead, we would store bits and pieces of the proximal stimulus. A good deal of the behavior of anterograde amnesiacs can be explained by saying that they lack a center for presenting a combined record of experience and context to working memory. As a result, they cannot recover memories of an experience when presented with contextual cues related to it.

It is one thing to say that a functional coordinating center must exist. It is quite another to explain how coordination and encoding take place. Although this is an active topic of current research, we cannot say that we understand either the physical or functional mechanisms involved.

In the case of the anterograde amnesiac, forgetting occurs because the experience-context link has never been placed in memory. In normal forgetting, the context cues associated with experience A, at time one, may be presented in association with experience B at time two. Subsequently, the context cues may be insufficient to recall A alone, but may recall B (erroneously) or some blend of A and B.

Retrieval is seen as a process of reconstructing memories associated with those cues that are present at retrieval time. Therefore, to facilitate memory for an event or fact, the processing of the stimulus situation during the retrieval period should be as close as possible to the processing that occurred when the original information was encoded. We can think of the retrieval of information from memory as an example of transferring previously established associations from one time and place to another. Memory will succeed if the memorizer is able to guess, at encoding time, what cues will be available at retrieval time, or to the extent that at retrieval time the memorizer is able to direct his or her attention to those cues that were processed at encoding time.

> *For an expanded discussion of the theoretical model, see Chapter 5/4Model.*

5.5 Application of the Model to Memory Phenomena

We next look at some selected memory phenomena not covered in earlier portions of the chapter. Here a brief description is given of each phenomenon. The main text gives a more complete description and, in some cases, applies the theoretical model just given to the phenomena being discussed.

Context effects refer to the surprising specificity of memory. Information acquired in one situation may be unretrievable in another, although the encoding and retrieval situations differ only on what observers (and experimenters) think are irrelevant dimensions. There are cases in which recognition memory for word lists can be reduced by using different type fonts in the encoding and recognition phases. There are other situations in which context-sensitive forgetting is a much more serious issue. Educators are only too familiar with students who learn how to apply mathematical concepts in the context of a science or mathematics classroom, yet utterly fail to apply the same concepts to problems in the world outside the class, such as calculating tips or, worse yet, to consumer credit management.

The general principle is that associations will be established between simultaneously presented, prominent cues. Nonprominent cues will be weakly associated with prominent ones, and will be subject to forgetting. Advertising can make use of these principles. If a message is presented in association with a prominently featured and a lightly featured cue, the less prominent cue may drop out of a reader or viewer's memory. This is particularly true for background information that is not presented as being relevant to the association the advertiser wants viewers to learn. Several studies have shown that if people repeatedly hear a message associating a candidate or product with a desired effect, they will retain the association between the product (candidate) and the effect, but will forget where they heard it. This is called *source amnesia*. If voters hear often enough that they should vote for Al because he's an honest man, then pretty soon, he may become "Honest Al" in the voters' minds. The voters forget that the advertisements defining Honest Al were sponsored by the Vote for Al Committee.

The concept of context extends to the context provided by a person's own body state. Studies have shown that when people have learned a fact when in a particular body state, memory will be improved if the body state can be reinstated at retrieval time. This principle has been illustrated with such diverse body state changes as being (or not being) underwater, being or not being mildly intoxicated with either alcohol or marijuana, and being or not being either happy or sad when information is to be memorized or retrieved.

Context can also refer to strictly psychological aspects of processing. In general, if the context in which information is memorized focuses attention on a variety of associations, memory will be improved. For example, suppose two people are presented with the same list of words. Person A is asked to generate rhymes for each word on the list, while person B is asked to generate semantic associates. Thus, if CAT was on the list, person A might have to think of BAT or SAT, whereas person B would have to think of DOG or KITTEN. Other things being equal, the person who generated the semantic associates will have a better memory for the original list than the person who generated the rhymes. This is known as the *depth of processing* effect. Although it is somewhat unsatisfactory as an explanatory principle, it is believed to work because the generation of semantic associates forces the memorizer to establish associations between a word and other words, and in the rhyming condition the memorizer can process the acoustic surface form of the word without establishing semantic associations.

The *encoding specificity* effect is closely related to depth of processing, but is usually used to demonstrate memory failures rather than memory successes. If a person thinks about an experience in a particular way (encodes it using a specific interpretation), the information is likely to be unavailable unless the retrieval context encourages the same sort of thinking. The principle can be illustrated in an artificial list learning situation. Suppose that a person learns a list containing the items BREAD, MEAT, BUTTER, EGGS, JAM, TOAST. Subsequently, the person is shown a list containing CAR, TRAFFIC, BRIDGE, JAM, HURRY, BUS, and is asked whether a word on the second list appeared on the first list. JAM is likely to be overlooked, because the implied semantic meaning of JAM was not the same on the two lists. It is of some interest that a similar principle, *functional fixedness*, has been demonstrated outside of the context of memory experiments. In a functional fixedness experiment a person is induced to use a tool in a particular way, such as using a pair of scissors to cut paper. Using a tool in the first way will reduce the probability that a person will realize that the same tool can be used in a different way, such as tying a pair of scissors to the end of a string to make a pendulum.

The reader may have noticed that most of the examples have been taken from laboratory work conducted in the Ebbinghaus tradition, where memory is studied in highly controlled settings. There are a few reports of analyses of memory in real world settings. A Dutch psychologist, Willem

Wagenaar, took careful notes on his own memory for everyday events for a period of several years. Wagenaar's (1986) observations were reassuringly compatible with the memory phenomena illustrated in more controlled settings. To learn something, focus on the cues that can be presented at retrieval time.

This has implications for education. Studying can be improved if, at study time, an individual tries to make sure that he or she has established associations between the material to be memorized and the cues that are likely to be present in the context in which retrieval is required.

One of the perennial questions in the study of memory, and for that matter cognition in general, has to do with children's learning. Both the behaviorist and information processing views of learning assume that the same processes are involved in children's learning and adult learning. The differences are due to children's having more to learn. The opposed view, sometimes called the *nativist* view, and more recently, *evolutionary psychology*, is that children are born with evolutionary determined hypotheses specifying permissible organizations of certain key aspects of the world. The child learns which of the evolutionary permitted organizations actually apply to the world that he or she lives in. It is important to realize that this argument applies only to learning of things that are central to human life, such as spoken language, elementary social structures, and perhaps a primitive sense of number. Everyone agrees that the "less important, less natural" organizing rules of a culture, such as reading, are acquired by exercising a general learning mechanism (Geary, 1995).

The nativist view has been advocated most vigorously by two of the most influential behavioral scientists of our times; Jean Piaget and Noam Chomsky. According to Piaget children go through genetically determined stages in which they use progressively more complicated logical rules for reasoning about the world. For example, according to Piaget, children under age two have difficulty understanding why an object is the same object if it is in view, then disappears behind an intervening (occluding) surface, and reappears on the other side of the occluding surface. Recent data suggest that Piaget undervalued the reasoning capabilities of very young children but the principle remains the same. Whereas we may use general learning and memory mechanisms to acquire information about culturally specific environments, children acquire information about local cultural solutions to obligatory problems, such as language definition or object permanence, through a process of hypothesis testing.

The argument for hypothesis testing, and by implication, evolutionary psychology, is even more developed in linguistics. Chomsky and others have argued that learning is a matter of *parameter setting*, where children learn which of several possible patterns are permitted in the language that their culture happens to speak. Phonetic rules provide particularly good examples of parameter setting. Well before they begin to speak, children have learned to be sensitive to the phonetic structure of their caregivers' language. It is hard to see how this could occur through a general learning mechanism, because the child acquires phonetic awareness before he or she begins to try out phonemes in speech.

The model developed in section 5 amounts to a general mechanism for memory and learning. Therefore, although it can accommodate all the other cases of memory phenomena cited in this section, it cannot accommodate the hypothesis-testing approach derived from the Chomsky's and Piaget's approach to children's learning. We have come to another of our big questions. By the standards of other species on this planet, humans are impressive general learners. Is it possible that those cognitions that are central to our ability to order the world, such as object permanence, language, and perhaps social relationships, are determined by evaluating hypothesis derived from evolution, rather than by applying our general learning capabilities to the world about us?

See Chapter 5/5SelectedPhenomena *for a considerably extended discussion of how the phenomena described here can be explained using the model of memory developed in Section 5/4.* Chapter 5/6Summary *provides a summarization of the arguments in the chapter.*

6

Visual-Spatial Representations

6.1 Overview

Primates, including humans, rely heavily on their vision and their ability to maintain spatial orientation. Applying Baddeley's (1986) model of primary memory, both visual orientation and visual reasoning are determined by the computational capacities of the visual-spatial scratchpad. In discussing them, we must break down visual-spatial thinking into several subcategories.

Visual perception deals with the transition from sensation to perception. *Visual reasoning* goes beyond visual perception by allowing us to imagine what a percept would look like if something were changed in the distal scene. This sort of reasoning turns out to be extremely important in a variety of human tasks, ranging from architecture to rearranging furniture. Psychological investigations try to characterize the transformations that we can imagine, and to locate the brain structures that support them.

Imagery can be thought of as visual reasoning without sensory support. Instead of creating a percept from the sensory stimulus we create one from memory. "Imagine a purple cow" illustrates the idea. More complex examples of imagery are easily developed. Experimentation has shown that there are some resemblances between the sorts of manipulations that can be made on percepts and images, but there are also significant differences. These are explored in subsequent sections in this chapter.

Spatial orientation involves representation of the space about us, and the related ability to reason about movement within that space. Although spatial orientation is not entirely dependent on the visual system, the two are closely linked.

There are two qualitatively different types of spatial representations: *Route representations* can be thought of as lists of directions of how to go from place to place (e.g., "on leaving the building, turn left and walk two blocks, then turn right"). *Configural representations* represent geographic information in a way that is akin to, but far from identical to, a "mental map" of an area. Both types of representation can be demonstrated in people and other animals.

Quite a lot is known about the neuroanatomy of visual-spatial reasoning. Recall that when an object is sensed, retinotopic maps are developed in the primary visual area, in the occipital lobe of the brain. The retinotopic information is used to develop object-relevant information, shape and color, processed in the ventral visual stream that extends into the temporal lobe. Information about location and movement is processed in the dorsal ventral stream, which is in the superior parietal lobe located at the middle-top of the brain. The information is put together again, in a manner that is as yet unknown, when these two streams are united in the frontal lobe. There are also many feedback loops, especially through the thalamus, a subcortical structure that seems to be involved in routing information from one area of the brain to another.

Popular psychology discussions sometimes make a great deal of the right brain–left brain distinction. In the extreme it is claimed that the left hemisphere is a serial processing device used for analytic reasoning and language, while the right hemisphere is a parallel-processing device that deals with intuitive reasoning and visual-spatial analyses. This is a great oversimplification. In chap. 2, I comment that different areas of the brain provide the tools for cognition. It is true that some specialized speech functions are located in the left hemisphere, and that visual analysis is done predominantly in the right hemisphere. The normal brain functions as a coordinated mechanism. Under normal circumstances, analytical linguistic and intuitive visual-spatial reasoning are produced by the integrated activity of several brain centers, on both sides of the brain.

An extended discussion of these points is provided in Chapter 6/1Overview.

6.2 Object and Scene Recognition

Imagine that you are looking at a complicated scene. Your eyes will make jumps from object to object, taking less than a tenth of a second to identify each of them. If an object is found that should not be there, such as a tractor

VISUAL-SPATIAL REPRESENTATIONS

in the midst of an underwater scene, your eyes begin to scan points close to the anomaly, for the brain–mind system evidently assumes that an anomaly in one region of a scene will be explained by information located nearby. Clearly, a great deal of computing is going on.

The visual system's ability to recognize orderly relations can be used to augment deficiencies in our ability to conduct formal reasoning. Mathematical and statistical relations that are hard to grasp when presented verbally or in equations can be made understandable by well-chosen diagrams. When choosing the diagrams, the illustrator has to decide what relation is to be stressed, and has to present it in a way that will be detected by normal visual processes.

More generally, we can view perception as a computational process where the goal is to locate identifiable objects, at known distances and bearings from the observer, by processing the information in the two-dimensional projections of the three-dimensional scene on the observer's retinas. The problem is a difficult one because different three-dimensional scenes can give rise to the same two-dimensional projection on the retina.

To solve the computational problem the perceptual system makes use of two types of cues: *Bottom-up cues* are developed by applying invariant information processing steps to visual information as it moves along the dorsal and ventral visual streams. *Top-down cues* are developed by conducting a preliminary analysis of visual input and then using that analysis to influence further processing. For example, the process of going from the punctate image on the retina to a collection of lines and curves is largely a bottom-up process. The process of interpreting lines, curves, and areas as surfaces associated with particular objects is subject to top-down influences. This is demonstrated in the main text (Fig. 6.12) by a collection of straight lines, curves, and circles that is initially perceived as a geometric design, but can be interpreted either as an olive falling into a stylized martini glass or a cartoon caricature of a woman wearing a bikini.

It is one thing to say that top-down and bottom-up processes interact to produce a percept. It is quite another to say how these interactions take place. The Gestalt psychologists, who believed that understanding perception was the key to understanding the mind, formulated a number of principles describing how geometric elements in a scene will be grouped together to form an interpretable scene. Examples of Gestalt principles are the rule that percepts are divided into a figure and a ground (loosely, the center of attention and the background), that points of light exhibiting synchronized movement will be seen as part of a single object, and that when two regions overlap the smaller will be seen as figure and the larger as ground.

The Gestalt principles are useful rules of thumb for describing a percept but they fail as explanations, because they provide no way of resolving conflicts when two or more of the principles lead us to different perceptions of the same scene. In fact, when this happens, the percept may shift back and forth between different interpretations of a scene.

In the late 1980s, David Marr, a computer scientist interested in machine vision, developed an influential computational account of image processing. Marr (1982) emphasized the detection of "non-accidental features" that would indicate the presence of a three-dimensional object, seen from a certain perspective. For instance, whenever three surfaces intersect in a scene, with the resulting corner pointing toward the observer, a "vertex" will appear in the two-dimensional projection of the scene (see Fig. 6.1). Therefore, block-like shapes can be detected by computing the relations between the vertex points. This illustrates only one of several non-accidental properties of the two-dimensional information on the retina that imply the presence of certain surface arrangements in the three-dimensional scene.

Marr's analyses showed how surprisingly far the visual system could go by using bottom-up processing alone. Nevertheless, top-down processes are important. This can be illustrated by showing that stylized pictures of familiar objects, such as faces, can be depicted quite easily against a normal background, provided that they are presented in their usual orientation. (In the case of faces, with the eyes above the nose and the nose above the mouth.) It is much harder to detect familiar objects when they are inverted. This fact presents a problem for any theory of exclusively bottom-up perception, because the phenomenon can be demonstrated using cartoon-like drawings in which the non-accidental properties are unchanged by inversion.

We conclude that perception depends on a complex interaction of bottom-up and top-down processes. Connectionist models have been developed to simulate top-down, bottom up interactions, using some of the techniques described to model interactions that were described in chap. 2. Although these models have yet to receive detailed verification, the fact that they work offers hope that the higher order perceptual processes will soon be understood through mathematical modeling.

If one takes an engineering perspective it is natural to try to build up the visual percept by the progressive development of complex cues from simple ones. Arrangements of dots in a two-dimensional projection of the three-dimensional world can be replaced by arrangements of lines, certain arrangements of lines can be used to infer edges in the three-dimensional world, surfaces can be inferred from edges, objects from surfaces, and so forth. In addition, it appears that primate vision depends on direct reac-

VISUAL-SPATIAL REPRESENTATIONS

tions to complicated cues present in the environment. For instance, gradients in surface texture are used to establish depth.

Texture is only one of several complex cues that appear to be perceived directly. Other directly perceivable cues make it possible to move around in the world. Fielders in games such as baseball and cricket use a variety of complicated geometric cues to position themselves to catch fly balls. The cues are used quite without any conscious awareness of them. In fact, the motor system can react correctly to visual cues that are interpreted incorrectly in the conscious percept. People can correctly position their fingers at the ends of vertical and horizontal lines that are equally long, although the vertical line appears to be considerably longer than the horizontal line.

While it has to be granted that some complex properties of the visual field are sensed directly, it is also likely that, in general, we locate and identify objects by using non-accidental properties building up progressively more complex descriptions. Marr (1982) referred to the analysis of a visual scene into non-accidental properties as a 2½ dimensional sketch, on the grounds that the collection of non-accidental properties provided evidence about the three dimensional structure of the environment, but did not quite define it. Marr's ideas have been extended by Irving Biederman (1995), who pointed out that to go beyond the 2½ dimensional sketch the mind can assume that the non-accidental properties in a scene were generated by collections of a limited number of prototypic three-dimensional geometric objects, which Biederman referred to as *geons*. The box-like shape in Fig. 6.1 is an example of such a geon. Others are presented in the main text, in *Chapter6\2Objects&Scenes*. The idea is that the non-accidental properties of the 2½ dimensional sketch permit the observer to infer the presence of geons viewed from a particular perspective. Any object becomes a collection of geons. For instance, a human torso could be described as a cylinder with smaller cylinders and cones attached. To see this, visualize the statue of Venus de Milo. The parameters of conic sections could be used to draw a computerized version of this famous artwork. The idea seems foreign to us, but after all, the problem for the brain is how to draw the computerized version. Interpretation and qualia come later.

Biederman's (1995) and similar approaches provide a way of explaining how we recognize classes of objects. Once the brain has inferred the presence of geons at particular locations in a scene an object can be described by the relation of its geons to each other. In the case of the Venus de Milo the statue is roughly described by a cylinder (the lower torso) topped by an inclined box-like figure (chest, with shoulders inclined). Two cones (the breasts) are attached to the box-like figure, and two long, narrow cylinders (the abbreviated arms) hang from the statue. This unartistic de-

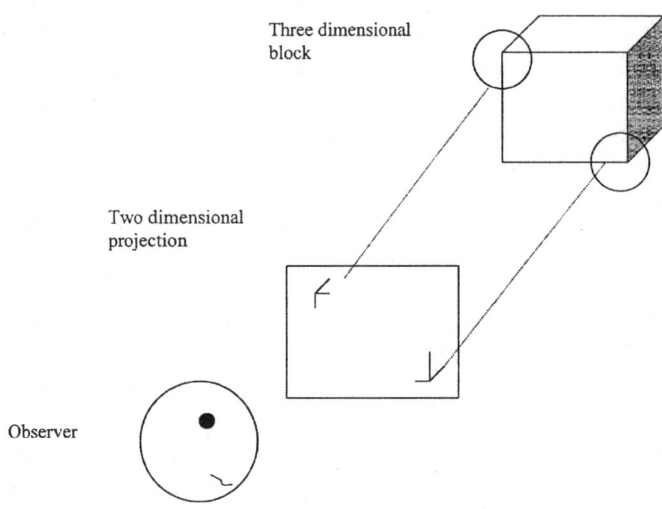

FIG. 6.1. Arrangement of surfaces in a three-dimensional scene will always result in the presence of characteristic vertices in the two-dimensional projection of the scene onto the retina. This information can be used by the observer's visual system to infer the presence of three-dimensional objects in the external world.

scription applies to any human female torso. The gist of Biederman's Recognition by Components (RBC) model is that we move from the 2½ dimensional sketch to a *geon structure descripton* (GSD) of objects. Objects can be assigned to classes (e.g., the Venus de Milo is recognized as a statue of a woman) once the GSD is determined. Note that this process works both with naturalistic representations, such as the *Venus* or an actual woman, and with highly stylized but still recognizable figures. Pictures of people taken from Picasso's cubist period do not look like any person who ever lived, but they are recognizable as people. The case of recognizing objects in naturalistic scenes is, if anything, much easier.

There is an interesting analogy between the Marr and Biederman approaches to perception and the modern technique of computer-aided design (CAD). In CAD geon-level descriptions of a scene are constructed, and then used to generate a point-by-point picture on a display device. Analyses such as Marr's and Biederman's depict visual processing as a reverse of CAD processing. The geon-level description is extracted from the retinotopic image on the primary visual cortex. The class of an object is recognized after its GSD has been determined. However, there is an alternative. It might be that GSDs are used indirectly, to sharpen the retinotopic information and to suggest candidate classes for the object being perceived. Prototypical images associated with the classes could then be generated from memory, and compared to the image derived from the object being perceived. According to this theory, the Venus de Milo, and with more difficulty, a cubist painting of a woman, are recognized because they look like previously experienced views of women.

These two approaches, which will be called *description-matching* and *image-matching*, differ in the importance that they assign to seeing things from a familiar direction. According to a pure theory of description matching, recognition should not depend on one's viewpoint, providing that all viewpoints being compared generate sufficient information in the image to generate the appropriate GSD. According to an image-matching approach recognition depends on matching the current percept to records of things seen before, and by definition, one's memory of things seen before is weighted toward seeing them from a familiar viewpoint. Unfortunately, the evidence on the importance of viewpoint is mixed. Although it would be nice to have a single theory of visual perception, it may be that the brain can use either description-matching or image-matching processes, depending on the circumstances.

Two-process theories can be accommodated within a reasonable model of the neuroanatomy of visual information processing. One such theory is sketched in the main text.

Chapter 6/2Objects&Scenes *contains an extended discussion of the concepts introduced here. This section also contains numerous examples of the sorts of perceptual processes discussed here.*

6.3 Transformations of a Visual Percept

Visual reasoning occurs when we look at something and decide something about a transformation of the scene. A good example is deciding that a suitcase will (or will not) fit into the trunk of a car, without actually trying to squeeze the suitcase in. Visual reasoning is actually a collection of related abilities. Chief amongst these are *visualization*, the ability to see if things will fit together without actually moving them (as in the suitcase example); *spatial rotation*, the ability to imagine movements of simple objects; *spatial orientation*, the ability to imagine how objects will appear from different perspectives; and *reasoning about movement*, the ability to reason about moving objects.

These different abilities were originally identified as part of research on intelligence testing (*psychometrics*). In the course of the study of intelligence, it has been found that in general, men do better than women on tests involving spatial rotations or reasoning about movement. Spatial reasoning also shows marked deterioration due to advancing age. Finally, neuropsychological studies have shown that spatial reasoning is sensitive to damage to the right hemisphere of the brain, whereas verbal reasoning is sensitive to damage in the left hemisphere. Visual-spatial reasoning is clearly a factor of intelligence, apart from either verbal ability or general intellectual ability.

Cognitive psychologists have contributed to the study of visual reasoning by showing that imagined movements in the mental space of the mind's eye obey constraints that are surprisingly close to physical constraints on actual movement. One of the most striking of such phenomena occurs when an observer is asked to make a same-different judgment about two objects seen at different orientations (e.g., a letter presented in its usual upright position and a letter presented at a 45° inclination from vertical). The time to make such judgments is a linear function of the angular difference in the orientations of the objects to be compared. This is surprising, because it suggests that if we are asked to imagine what something would look like if it were at a different position or orientation we successively imagine it moving through all the spaces on the path between the two positions. Clearly, this would be a requirement for actual movement; if we push a piece of furniture from one position to another along the floor it will occupy every point along its route. But why shouldn't objects jump from place to place in mental space?

The fact is that they do not. On the other hand, the constraints that apply to imagined movement are not exactly the constraints applied by physics. In some cases, the path an (imagined) object takes is constrained to the path that can be constructed from successive rotations and translations. In other cases, the path taken through mental space seems constrained by higher order interpretations of the visual scene. For instance, suppose that a person views successive displacements of a pointed design labeled "rocket ship." The observer will tend to imagine that the object is traveling upward at a constant velocity. If the same pattern is labeled as a "steeple," the imagined motion is in the downward direction.

More details concerning transformations of a percept can be found in Chapter 6/3 Transformations.

6.4 Imagery

Imagery is the construction of an internal "percept" based on information in memory. The percept may be of a previous experience, or it may be constructed by combining memorized information, as a person would have to do if asked to imagine a purple cow. Historically there has been a great deal of interest in the role of imagery in thought. The topic is a difficult one to investigate simply because of the subjective nature of the phenomenon. We can compare two tourists' snapshots of their visit to the Grand Canyon, but we cannot compare their images.

Many experiments have tried to develop the relationship between imagery and perception. In a typical study, people are asked to perform some task using imagery or using an actual perceptual display. For instance, a person might be asked, in an imagery condition, whether the angle between the large and small hands of an analog clock is greater at 3:20 or 12:35. In the perception condition, the observer would make this judgment by viewing actual analog clocks. Imagery is inferred to be like perception, if the relation between the actual angles and the speed and accuracy of judgments are the same in the imagery and perceptual conditions.

Stephen Kosslyn (1980, 1983, 1984), a professor at Harvard University, has conducted an extensive series of experiments of this sort to understand the functional characteristics of imaging. His work can be thought of as an attempt to specify operational limits on the visual-spatial scratchpad in Baddeley's (1986) model of working memory. Kosslyn (1983) drew the following conclusions about the image, and hence the scratchpad:

1. *The imaged field is limited in scope.* Just as we can only see so much at a time, we are also restricted in our ability to image.

2. *The imaged field is functionally continuous.* (Note that this is consistent with the conclusion that things do not jump from place to place in the mind's eye.)

3. *Attention is limited.* Detection of detail is greatest in the center of the imaged field, and falls off rapidly from the center.

4. *Images are generated part by part, and roughly in the order in which attention would be moved across a visual scene.*

These are rather bold assertions, based on experiments in which observers are asked either to scan a scene to detect a feature or to image the same scene and try to detect the feature. In general, these experiments show similar effects; the variables that make a feature easy or hard to detect in an actual visual scene operate in the same way in an imaged scene. There are three exceptions to this general statement. First, imaging effects are usually smaller than perceptual effects. Second, reaction times in imaging experiments can be almost half a second longer than reaction times in equivalent perceptual studies. Third, it appears that the images are built up piece by piece, whereas visual percepts are constructed in parallel.

The strong analogies between the results of studies of imaging and perception could be explained by assuming that when a person images, the brain mechanisms for perception take their input from memory, rather than from the sensory system. This has been called a "back-projection" model of imagery. The hypothesis that imaging and perception use the same brain mechanisms has been reinforced by studies showing that imaging while a person is looking at a scene can influence perception of that scene. Furthermore, the effect occurs at a fairly low level of perception—detection of black lines projected on a gray background. To understand the interaction between perception and imagery more clearly we need to look at a formal theory of imagery, constructed to account for behavioral evidence, and consider how this theory accords with neuroscientific observations.

The neuroscientific data generally supports the back-projection model. Cases have been reported in which brain-injured patients lose the ability to draw from memory, although retaining the ability to draw from a model. Such cases usually have damage to the left posterior temporal region, which is not part of the visual analysis system. This suggests that the left posterior temporal region either stores or generates images that are then placed on the primary visual cortex for further analysis. Damage to the primary visual cortex usually produces analogous damage to imaging. For instance, damage to the right hemisphere's primary visual cortex reduces or eliminates conscious perception in the left visual field. It also reduces or eliminates the ability to image objects that would be located in the left visual field, were they to be present physically. Similarly, damage to regions involved in the ventral or dorsal visual streams seem to produce analogous deficiencies in the ability to see and image either object information (if the ventral stream has been damaged) or location information (if the dorsal stream has been damaged). These findings from neuropsychology are beginning to be supported by findings from neuroimaging, that show activity in many of the same brain regions during either perception or imaging.

However, a note of caution is in order. Although the back-projection model is a good broad survey of the literature there are several studies that do not fit with it. The reasons for the discrepancy are unclear. The topic of

VISUAL-SPATIAL REPRESENTATIONS 85

imagery is currently under active discussion, so it is reasonable to suppose that we shall have a detailed understanding of imagery in the near future.

Readers interested in imagery should look carefully at the more detailed descriptions in Chapter 6/4Imagery.

6.5 Spatial Orientation

6.5.1- 6.5.4 Conceptual and Methodological Issues

Spatial Orientation refers to the development of an awareness of the space around us. *Wayfinding* is a special case in which we find routes from one point to another. Spatial orientation is a problem to be solved, not an elementary function of the mind. Various species have developed different techniques for solving those orientation problems that are important to them. Some of these, such as the salmon's use of chemical sensors to locate its spawning stream, tell us little about human spatial orientation. In other cases, though, the study of orientation in laboratory animals has proven very instructive for understanding human orientation. This is probably because many, if not all, mammals have similar species-general brain mechanisms for orientation. Note the plural form; mammals have and use different techniques for maintaining orientation. Rats, for instance, use different strategies in different situations. Humans display the same sort of opportunism.

Cross-cultural studies provide a dramatic picture of how many approaches there are to spatial orientation. Modern city-dwellers think of their cities in terms of a hierarchy of districts and neighborhoods, characterized by familiar landmarks. Polynesian and Micronesian navigators, faced with the challenge of navigating in the open sea, developed an elaborate reference system based on star patterns. The Polynesians did not have a modern astronomer's understanding of the Earth's motion relative to the sky, but did have a system that converted the trackless ocean into a plane with celestial signposts hanging over it. The forest-dwelling Fang hunters of Equatorial Guinea have yet another way of maintaining orientation. They rely on local landmarks, maintain orientation by noting whether they are going up or down a mountain, and use their own sense of fatigue as a way of estimating distance. These three very different methods of wayfinding all work for the environment in which they are used.

Humans both solve orientation problems at the individual level and communicate the solutions to other people. To do this, we have to develop a way of talking about space. One way to do this is to develop an absolute reference system, such as the modern latitude–longitude system. It applies anywhere on Earth, providing that the navigator is trained to use it and has access to the appropriate instruments. At the other extreme, some cultures used routes based on directions up and down a mountain, and distances measured partly by the physical effort expended on a journey.

In addition to using absolute reference systems, humans use a variety of *relative* reference systems, in which distances and directions are specified relative to a prominent or strategically located object. One of the most psychologically important of these is the *egocentric* system, in which relative locations (direction and distance) are specified relative to the wayfinder. In addition, the location of object A may be specified relative to object B. This will be called an *intrinsic* frame of reference. When thinking about space, people freely switch from different types of representations. For instance, when giving directions, a person may include an egocentric reference, references to objects, and absolute references such as "Look to the South." The flexibility of reference is a further illustration of how powerful and opportunistic the brain–mind system of spatial orientation can be.

Certain generalizations can be made about how people develop knowledge of a space. In general, they progress from awareness of landmarks to knowledge of the routes between landmarks, then to configural knowledge about the location of points in an absolute or relative reference system. This is sometimes referred to as the progression from landmark recognition to route knowledge, and then to the development of a cognitive map. Although these are useful metaphors, we must remember that the progression is not inevitable, that people will switch back and forth between types of representation depending on the sort of task that they are asked to do and, most importantly, that the term "cognitive map" should not be taken too literally. There are significant and systematic differences between the configural information represented in an actual map and the configural information held in the mind.

The term *spatial orientation* has been used to refer to knowledge of many different types of spaces. These include visual scenes immediately before the wayfinder, the surrounding space, including the space behind the observer, a neighborhood through which a wayfinder moves, and large-scale geographic spaces, such as the United States, that can only be experienced through the interpretation of artifacts, such as maps. I suggest that these different spaces be kept separate, for different psychological processes are required to understand each type of space.

We turn next to a methodological question. Suppose a person has developed a representation of some space, and as experimenters, we wish to know what it is. One way to find out is to ask the person to describe or draw the space. Such direct reports have a good deal of face validity, but they simultaneously evaluate the respondent's knowledge of the space and his or her skill in description and drawing. Inaccuracies in either an account or a drawing may be due to inaccuracies in knowledge of the space or an inability to describe (or draw) it accurately. Therefore, two alternative approaches have been taken. One is to have the respondent perform some task, such as moving through the environment or pointing to unseen objects, where the behavior is easy to perform. This technique is called *convergence*. When convergence reveals discrepancies between where the respondent thinks objects are located and where they actually are, the inaccuracies can be assigned to the respondent's mental representation rather than to an inability to perform the task.

In the second alternative approach, *Multidimensional scaling* (MDS), the respondent is asked to compare distances between two points. For instance, a person might be asked if the distance from San Francisco to Los Angeles is greater than or less than the distance from New York to Washington, DC. Computer-intensive techniques are then used to find a configuration of locations in a two or three-dimensional Euclidean space that will satisfy the respondent's judgments. This method of externalizing a person's cognitive map has become quite popular with experimenters, because of its mathematical elegance and because people can produce a large number of pairwise judgments of distance within a short period of time.

Experimenters who use either convergence, or MDS, techniques compare the map (more precisely, configuration of object locations) produced by a respondent's judgments to an actual configuration of locations in physical space. When this comparison is made, an important philosophical distinction must be kept in mind. The comparison is not between actual spatial locations and the respondent's mental model of those locations; it is between actual locations and the experimenter's estimate of what the respondent's mental model is. If the experimenter's techniques for constructing the estimate rely on unjustified assumptions, the estimate may not be accurate.

In particular, convergence and MDS techniques are based on the assumption that the respondent is reporting measurements taken in a (mental) space that obeys certain principles known as the *metric axioms*. Euclid's axioms are a special case of the metric axioms. For example, the metric axioms include the assumption that the distance from point A to point B is the same as the distance from point B to point A. Although this is true in our everyday Euclidean space, there is no reason that it be true in mental space. In fact, some experiments to be discussed below indicate that mental representations of space are not metric. To see why this might be so, consider how a taxi driver might represent space in a city that has many one-way streets. If the driver's mental representation is established by the time it takes to go from one point to another, instead of the distance traversed, the driver's mental representation will not be metric.

Two approaches have been used to uncover non-metric properties of mental spaces. One is to see if a person can piece together separately traveled paths to produce a novel path from one point to another. This evaluates a person's representation of connectivity between points, a topographic rather than a metric property. The other technique is to find clusters of points that the respondent sees as belonging together, without making the stronger assumption that belonging together is a metric relationship. This method can be used to establish hierarchies of points, such as states within a region, cities within a state, and neighborhoods within a city. One method, semantic priming, has the interesting property of relying on implicit rather than explicit judgments of closeness. Therefore, it can be used to evaluate implicit as well as declarative memory for spatial information.

With these methodological properties aside, we move to a discussion of substantive findings on how people represent spatial information.

For a further, expanded discussion of the variety of ways in which people represent space, and the methodological and philosophical issues involved in studying these representations, see Chapter 6/5SpatialReasoning/1-4Introduction.

6.5.5 Surrounds

A *surround* is the space immediately about a person (i.e., the space that a person can observe by rotation without translation). As common sense leads us to believe, observers are normally most aware of objects to their immediate front. We are also more aware of, and quicker to locate, objects that are above us than those below us, and objects that are immediately behind us rather than to our side. There are cases where this pattern changes. If an observer is told to indicate the direction to an object with respect to an orienting object, then the observer is most aware of objects close to the orienting object even if the orienting object is off to the side. Also, if an observer learns about a surround from a map or diagram instead of from direct experience, then the direction of the orienting object is important. Responding is quickest when the orienting object is straight up (North, in the conventional presentation of maps), and decreases as the orienting object moves away from a straight-up position on the map.

Logically, there are two ways in which people might store information about surrounds. One would be to store configural information about the relation of objects to each other at the time the surround was explored. This strategy of memorization is an example of *early computation*. If early computation is used, all information required to answer a question about the position of object A relative to object B is already in memory. Therefore, if a person is asked how a surround looks from a particular perspective, the person can answer equally well whether that perspective has actually been experienced. If the observer is using a *late computation* strategy, he or she stores a series of perspective views and answers questions by reinstating these views, and if necessary, computing configural information from them. If late computation is used an observer should answer questions about how a surround looks from an experienced perspective more rapidly than he or she can answer questions about how it looks from an unexperienced perspective. Whether an observer uses early or late computation depends on precisely what tasks the observer has to accomplish during the learning stage. This reinforces the general principle that the spatial information a person acquires depends on how that person interacts with a space during the learning phase. It is also a useful reminder that the brain–mind system can approach a seemingly basic task, maintaining spatial orientation, in two different ways.

More information concerning surrounds, together with a description of some of the key experiments, can be found in Chapter 6/5SpatialReasoning/5Surrounds.

By definition, neighborhoods consist of collections of surrounds that can be linked together by traversing routes. Thus, although my office is a surround, the building in which it is located and the campus in which the building is located, are neighborhoods.

A wayfinder needs to know two types of information about a neighborhood; the routes that connect one point to another and the way in which key locations and routes are embedded in the three-dimensional space occupied by a neighborhood. I will refer to route information and configural information. *Route information* mainly has to do with connectivity, which is a topographic rather than a metric property of a set of points in a space. However, certain types of route learning make sense only if the wayfinder assumes that the route is embedded in a Euclidean space. *Configural information* is, by definition, metric information. In the extreme, a person who has complete configural knowledge of a set of locations should be able to associate each location with its coordinates in a Euclidean system.

Some routes can be followed by *tracking* (i.e., following prestablished signs that mark the route). Tracking has the advantage of being simple and rapid. It has the disadvantage that a tracker may learn very little about the route itself, and hence be unable to repeat a traverse if the tracking signs are eliminated.

Dead reckoning is a method of route following that is in some way the logical antithesis of tracking. Dead reckoners keep track of the turns and distances of the segments they traverse as they travel along a route. This record provides enough information so that the dead reckoner can return directly to any point previously visited, without retracing steps in the way that a tracker would have to do. When humans use dead reckoning, they regard it as a rather sophisticated strategy. For instance, prior to the development of reliable clocks deep-sea sailors kept track of their position by dead reckoning. To do this they either graphed their position on charts or solved problems in trigonometry. (During the 18th and early 19th centuries, one of the duties of captains in the Royal Navy was to instruct the midshipmen in trigonometry!) Dead reckoning is not the sole province of trained navigators, although dead reckoning over great distances may be. Dead reckoning can be demonstrated over courses of tens of meters in the laboratory. In fact, some species of nonhuman animals, including the desert ant and the dog, are capable of dead reckoning over short distances.

Psychologically, the main challenge facing a dead reckoner is to keep track of turns and distances traveled. Turns can be sensed directly, although there is a tendency for people to square off turns, moving them toward the nearest right angle. Once turned, the dead reckoner, and the pilot discussed next, has to be able to maintain bearing. A wayfarer can maintain bearing by observing *optic flow*, the apparent acceleration of objects off a wayfarer's route as the wayfarer moves by them. The only objects that do not exhibit optic flow are objects on the route. Optic flow can also be used as an indicator of the wayfarer's speed. Estimated speed and estimated time can be combined to estimate distance.

Piloting may be the commonest technique for route following. Pilots represent routes as a series of control points and turns to be taken when a control point is reached. Thus, a tourist might receive the piloting instructions "Walk out of the front door of the hotel, turn left, and walk until you reach the castle." Wayfinders who rely on piloting do not need to estimate distances, but they do need to know how to maintain bearing and recognize control points when they reach them.

Recent neuroscientific studies of the rat have shown that place recognition apparently takes place in the hippocampus. Cells in the thalamus are sensitive to the direction in which the rat points its head. Connectionist modeling has shown how these two sources of information could be hooked together to form a route-map. There is at least a suggestion that something like this happens in humans. In one study, London taxi drivers were asked to recall routes while their brains were being imaged. Route recall was associated with increased metabolic activity in the hippocampal and parahippocampal regions. Hippocampal activity did not increase when the drivers were asked to recall places they had visited on their vacation, such as the Statue of Liberty, that were memorable sites but were not on the usual route of a London cabby.

When people are trying to follow routes, they will freely mix up tracking, dead reckoning, and piloting. There is nothing wrong with saying "To get to the Lincoln Memorial from the White House, follow signs to the Washington Memorial, turn right, and walk about a quarter mile."

Configurational learning is considered to be the most powerful representation of space. A *configuration* is a collection of nodes, plus the distances between nodes and set of all the angles {<BAC} between locations B and C, measured at point A. If the distances between angles conform to the metric axioms discussed earlier, then each location within a configuration can be treated as a coordinate point in a metric space. In such spaces, distances between any two points x,y are computed by the equation:

$$d(x,y) = (\Sigma_{(i=1,n)} |x_i - y_i|^r)^{1/r}$$

where n is the dimensionality and r > 0 is the *Minikowski parameter* of the space. The familiar two-dimensional Euclidean space of a conventional map is a metric space with n = 2 and r = 1.

A configuration is invariant over translation and origin (i.e., the origin point and the direction chosen to be the 0° bearing are arbitrary). Conventional maps, though, have specified origins and bearings. Therefore, to coordinate a configural representation with a map a wayfinder has to define the initial position of a route, either by starting from location of known position or by dead reckoning from such a position. In addition, the wayfinder has to align direction in the representation with direction on the ground. Once the initial positioning and alignment problems are solved, the positions of all other points on a route can be determined by dead reckoning. In addition, triangulation can be used to find the position of any off-route location, providing that the wayfinder knows the bearings from at least two on-route locations to the off-route location.

Because configurations are invariant over translation and rotation, pointing tasks, in which the respondent describes relative bearings from point A to point C, relative to point B (i.e., the angle < BAC) provide a way of determining the extent to which a person's cognitive representation of a configuration matches the configuration measured on the ground. It turns out that, on the average, people can estimate angles to within about 20°. Individual differences are quite large, so the average value is misleading. In addition, errors are systematic. As was the case in route learning, there is a tendency to square off angles, by recalling them as being closer to a right angle than they were.

If we are willing to assume that a person's configural representation is equivalent to positioning objects in a metric space, then we can use the MDS technique to uncover a mental configuration. This procedure takes the mental map metaphor very strongly indeed, and is probably unjustified, for distance estimates show systematic departures from the metric axioms. Mental spaces appear to be ordered hierarchically into small regions, and then larger regions that contain smaller ones. Points within the same region tend to be thought of as closer to each other than they are in physical space, whereas points in different regions tend to be thought of as being further apart. This distortion can cause a set of distance judgments to violate the metric axioms. Under certain circumstances, distances will be seen as being asymmetric (i.e., the distance from point A to point B will be judged as being less than the distance from point B to point A). This is especially likely to happen if point A is a prominent, well known landmark, and point B is a less well known location in the vicinity of A.

It has been suggested that asymmetries in distance judgments are a special case of asymmetries in similarity judgments, in which the resemblance of item A to item B is not equal to the resemblance of B to A. In fact, asymmetries in both spatial distances and similarities can be derived from the same model of the comparison process. Whatever the reason, the fact that there are spatial asymmetries is important, because they represent a flagrant violation of the metric axioms. For this reason, it may be preferable not to consider mental space at all. Instead, perhaps we should just say that under some circumstances people learn enough about a space so that they can make decisions (e.g., pointing) that require access to configural information.

A considerably more detailed discussion of experiments about how people develop representations of their neighborhoods can be found in Chapter 5/5SpatialReasoning/6-7 Neighborhoods.

6.5.8 Individual Differences

Spatial orientation abilities vary widely across people. Children below the age of 10 or 12 seem to have difficulty in learning an environment, either due to inattention or to a poor selection of landmarks. By early adolescence children give essentially adult-like performance. At the other end of the life span, aged individuals, on the average, show reduced spatial orientation performance. However, this may be due to other illnesses (e.g., Alzheimer's Disease) that are concomitants of aging, rather than being due to

VISUAL-SPATIAL REPRESENTATIONS

the normal aging process itself. Some elderly individuals retain considerable spatial orientation skill into their sixties and seventies.

Male–female differences in spatial orientation have been widely publicized. Most of the data is based on superior male performance on paper and pencil tests said to measure spatial orientation, rather than field observations of orienting behavior. Nevertheless, a few studies have observed wayfinding directly, and these studies do find that, on average, men do better than women. This seems to be at least partially due to strategies. Men report observing environments in a way that would lead them to acquire configural information, whereas women report strategies of observation that facilitate route learning. Once again, it should be stressed that there are wide differences in orienting ability within men and women, as well as a consistent male–female difference.

At least some of the individual differences in spatial orientation are due to strategies, for training programs certainly work. Alternately, the fact that striking losses of performance are associated with a genetic abnormality (Turner's syndrome), and the persistent male–female difference in orienting ability suggests that the differences may be partly due to individual differences in physiological processes. Untangling these issues is a topic for future research.

See Chapter 6/5SpatialReasoning/8IndividualDifferences *for a further discussion of these issues.*

6.9 Artifacts

A great deal of our learning about spaces comes from secondary sources. We consider three such sources: maps, verbal descriptions, and exploration of virtual spaces generated by computers (virtual environments). The use of each of these artifacts brings with it significant psychological challenges.

Maps. There are two broad categories of maps, perspective maps and plan-view maps. Perspective maps are cartoonlike characterizations of how a scene or journey might look from the wayfinder's point of view. These maps are easy to interpret, and children actually prefer them to plan-view maps. However, plan-view maps can represent more information in an extremely compact notation. This comes at a not-inconsiderable expense, for it is not easy to learn to read plan-view maps. Abstract codes for ground features, such as representing height by contour lines, are particularly hard to comprehend. However, once the talent for map-reading has been acquired, map study can actually be more informative than exploration. This is especially true if the goal is to acquire configural information about a neighborhood, for plan-view maps emphasize configurations.

However, plan-view maps do have their handicaps. The first has already been mentioned, the map-reader has to be able to interpret an abstract code. In addition, the map-reader has to be able to establish correspondences between his or her own position and line of sight on the ground and positions and bearings on the map. This is best done by holding a map so that "up" on the paper corresponds to "forward" on the ground. Finally, memories for maps will be distorted. In particular, there is a tendency to regularize lines on the map, so that political boundaries and lines corresponding to geographic features (e.g., rivers, coastlines) are remembered as running more North–South or East–West than they actually do. (Despite its name and latitude, South America is not directly south of North America.)

Language. Language can be used to describe spatial arrangements. When this is done, a comprehender has to develop a mental model of a space from propositions expressed in a text. The model might simply be a list of propositions explicitly stated in the text, it might contain (some of) these propositions and a small number of immediate inferences from them, or it might be a spatial model of the situation, similar to the one that would have been constructed if the comprehender had experienced the situation being described. The choice of a model will determine how easily questions about the situation can be answered. If the model contains the answer to a question, then it can simply be read out from memory. In general, though, the more information placed into a model as the text is presented, the greater the burden on early computation processes. If the model of the text contains information from which the answer can be inferred, then late computation can be used.

People who go to the trouble of imaging surrounds as they are described (i.e., accept a heavy early computation burden), answer questions about object locations in much the same way that they would have had they actually been in the space in question. Objects that were described as being in front of the observer are recalled most rapidly, next objects to the back, and finally, objects to the side. Objects described as being above the observer are recalled more quickly than objects described as being below the observer. Finally, if a surround is described from multiple perspectives, comprehenders merge the descriptions into a single memory of a surround.

When texts are used to describe neighborhoods, the model that comprehenders develop may either emphasize configural or route information, depending on how the text is constructed. Route learning seems to be preferred. Although comprehenders can answer questions about both connectivity and configural relations depending on how the space has been described to them, they evidently do not construct mental images of the space that they know only from text.

Descriptions show a similar flexibility; how people describe a space depends on how they have experienced it and what they think the listener needs to know. Surrounds are generally described by taking the reader–listener on a "gaze tour," describing what the comprehender would see if he or she were actually there. Neighborhoods that the describer knows only by maps are usually described in configurational terms. Neighborhoods that the describer knows from personal experience are usually described in route terms. As in the case of the description of a surround, the describer tries to take the listener into the situation. However, descriptions can be altered to emphasize route or configurational knowledge if the describer thinks this best meets the listener's needs.

The previous statements imply that the speaker has a great deal of flexibility in describing a space. That is not entirely true. The ability to describe spaces is related to (psychometrically defined) visual-spatial reasoning. In general, the higher the reasoning ability the greater facility a person has in using configural terminology. Women tend to give route descriptions more than do men, which is consistent with observed differences in the way that men and women comprehend spatial settings. Finally, the speaker–listener's language may be important. Natural languages vary in the richness of their terms for spatial descriptions. People whose linguistic experience is confined to the modern European languages, and especially English, may not appreciate this. English, the other Germanic languages, and the Romance languages have a relatively rich lexicon for spatial relations. There are situations where a speaker's native language constrains his or her ability to describe a spatial situation.

Virtual Environments. Virtual environments (VEs) are computer-generated displays that attempt to place the observer into an environment defined solely by the computer's database. For instance, in principle, one could explore a house that had not yet been built by placing the architect's plans into a computer database, and then "moving through" the house by using a virtual environment program. The technology is quite new, but enough experimentation has been done with it to establish its utility and illustrate some of the problems it poses.

Desktop VE represents spaces by presenting scenes on a conventional computer display unit. The scenes are shown as they would appear if an observer manipulated a vehicle moving through an environment. Motion is indicated by a conventional computing interface, such as a keyboard or an electronic mouse. *Immersive VE* attempts to simulate actual exploration by enclosing the observer's head so that only the virtual environment can be seen, and by using devices such as head movements, and occasionally, foot movements, to provide at least a minimal simulation of natural motion through the environment. Caves are room-sized environments in which computer-generated scenes are projected on a wall. The computer detects the observer's motion by tracking special sensing devices placed on the observer's clothing, and adjusts the scene accordingly.

Within the limits of the technology, object shape cues are identical in both real and virtual environments. (Current technology places the observer in what is best described as a cartoon world, but this situation will undoubtedly improve as better equipment is constructed.) Some, but not all, of the cues to object distance can be simulated in a virtual environment. Indeed, some of them can be enhanced. It is more difficult to simulate the observer's own motion.

Despite these differences between perception in real and virtual environments, it appears that either can be used to develop a cognitive representation of an environment. In fact, quite reasonable representations can be developed by experience with desktop VE, although this represents, rather than simulates, actual experience with an environment. For some reason that is not clearly understood, women seem to have much more trouble developing spatial representations in virtual environments than do men. The male–female contrast in virtual environment studies is much greater than the contrast in comparable studies involving real environments.

In summary, it is clear that people can use artifacts, maps, narratives, and virtual environments to develop a representation of a space that they have never visited. This emphasizes an important point: Developing a configural representation of a space is a controlled, cognitive act. This contrasts with development of route knowledge, which may be partially based on procedural knowledge.

For more discussion of the use of artifacts to develop representations of space, see Chapter 6/5SpatialOrientation/9Artifacts.

The discussion of Spatial Orientation is summarized in Chapter 6/5SpatialOrientation/10Summary. *For a summary of the findings concerning visual-spatial reasoning, see* Chapter 6/6Summary.

7
Language and Thought

7.1 Introduction

The power of human language far exceeds the power of communication systems used by other animals. We use language to express ideas, whereas other animals use signals to express emotions. Any essay on human thought has to deal with the role of language. In doing so, we deal with three subquestions: How language should be described, how the brain and mind are organized to deal with language, and how the form of language influences the form of thought.

Remarks about language and its effects appear in Greek and Roman texts. Formal programs for the study of language began in Europe in the 17th and 18th centuries. These programs, and especially the activities of the Port Royal Grammarians in France, established a tradition of linguistic analysis that is alive today, the active study of language as a system of rules for generating expressions. A second tradition of linguistics, the description of different languages, can be traced to the 18th-century discovery of commonalities between languages as widely separated in time and space as Sanskrit, an ancient language of India, and modern English. Studies in this tradition have resulted in a categorization of languages into groups of related languages, and have been compared to groupings of people on the basis of genetic analyses. More controversially, some descriptive linguists have speculated about the influence that the form of a person's native language has over his or her thoughts. This is known as the Sapir-Whorf hypothesis, combining the names of its two most famous proponents.

To begin the discussion, we look at the approach of linguists, who study how language can be described as a formal, symbol-manipulating system. We also discuss the psychogical issues that may arise when people attempt to deal with this system.

> *For an expansion on the introductory remarks, and a discussion of some of the history of linguistics, see* Chapter 7/1 Introduction.

7.2 Language as a Formal System

Linguists define a language as the set of all expressions native speakers judge to be acceptable. "Acceptable" here means grammatically acceptable, rather than sensible. The expression, *The rabbit calculated Einstein's desire for boiled eggs* is grammatically acceptable English, although what it means is a bit unclear. Acceptable expressions are formed by assembling lexical items (loosely, words) into an expression in accordance with a set of syntactical rules. Such expressions are said to be well formed. The syntactical structure of the expression determines the dependency relations between the lexical terms in that particular expression. Semantic analysis is used to determine what an expression means. This is done by combining the meaning of the lexical terms, as references to extra-linguistic concepts, with the dependency relations between terms specified by the syntactic analysis. As a result, we understand that *John loves Mary* and *Mary loves John* are quite different statements.

In all languages that have been investigated, the syntactical rules are sufficient to generate an infinite number of different sentences from the finite set of lexical terms. However there are limits on the complexity of comprehendible sentences. To see this, consider the successive expressions:

> The rat ate the cheese.
> The rat the cat chased ate the cheese.
> The rat the cat the dog scared chased ate the cheese.
> The rat the cat the dog the man owned scared chased at the cheese.

We can reach incomprehensibility without violating the syntactical rules of English. This example illustrates the difference between the competence and performance of a speaker and a language. *Competence* refers to the set of expressions that can be generated by applying the syntactic rules of a language to a lexicon. *Performance* refers to a speaker's ability to use ex-

LANGUAGE AND THOUGHT

pressions. Competence is determined by the structure of the language; performance is determined by the structure of the language and the computational capabilities of a speaker's mind.

Comprehension and communication do not stop when syntactic and semantic analyses are completed. An expression may have quite a different meaning as a part of a discourse than it does considered as an isolated sentence. This is illustrated by polite requests, as in *Can you pass the salt?* Determining the meaning of an expression in context is called *pragmatic analysis*. Expressions also have to be incorporated into discourses, which follow their own structure. This can be seen by contrasting the structures of mystery novels, scientific articles, and sermons. At this level, linguistics has moved into the psychological topic of discourse analysis.

There has been, and is, a continuous debate over the extent to which language is a special property of the brain–mind system, with its own rules for learning and use, compared to the extent to which linguistic behavior can be derived from general psychological laws of learning and cognition. Some linguists take the extreme position that this debate has been settled. To understand what the debate is about, we need to take a close look at the way in which linguists think of the relation between language and thought.

Generative linguistic theory assumes that thoughts are generated in an internal language, sometimes referred to as *mentalese*. For many purposes, mentalese can be regarded as being equivalent to a statement in the predicate calculus. (There are some cases in which natural language statements do not translate easily into the calculus notation, but these will be ignored for the moment.) From a linguist's point of view, a language is explained when the rules are stated for transforming a statement from the internal mentalese to an external *surface structure* sentence. A linguist does this by going from the species-general propositional form to a language-specific, *deep structure* form. In English, for instance, this would be the simple subject–verb–object order, plus markers to indicate whether the statement was to be expressed as a question, a passive form, or some other form requiring a special ordering. Various transformations are then applied to derive the external expression, or *surface form*, from the deep form.

Generative grammar theory formally describes this process. The basic elements of generative grammar theory are a *lexicon* consisting of *terminal* symbols, which can be thought of as words or morphemes, and *nonterminal* symbols, or grammatical categories. The initial deep structure form consists of the single nonterminal S, for 'sentence' or 'expression.' A finite set of *syntactical rules* constitute the grammar of a language. Each syntactic rule describes a possible writing from one string of lexical symbols to another. A *language* is the set of expressions that can be generated starting at S. For example, the rule, S -> NounPhrase (NP) Verb (V) NounPhrase (NP), expresses the idea that an expression can take the form

NP V NP. Eventually, we reach terminal symbols. To illustrate, if we add the rules NP -> Article (A) Noun (N) and, to allow some terminals, A -> *the*, N -> *cat*, N -> *dog*, V -> *saw*, we generate a language with just two sentences; *The cat saw the dog*, and *The dog saw the cat*. Of course, the grammars and lexicons of actual languages are much more complicated.

Syntactical rules do not simply substitute one term for another, in an invariant order, until a string of terminal symbols is produced. Every language contains some rules that can be applied recursively, which means that there is no maximum length for an expression. Therefore, the set of well-formed expressions is infinite, although a native speaker can interpret any of them. This fact was one of the objections that Chomsky levied against Skinner's associationist interpretation of language use. Chomsky argued that novel sentences could not possibly be interpreted by generalization from previously learned sentences. Instead, Chomsky argued that language learners must have incorporated and applied the rules of syntax to determine dependency relations between lexical elements in an expression (i.e. which was the subject, which was the object, and so forth). Once dependency relations were known, semantic meanings were substituted to determine the meaning of the expression. Since Chomsky's original work, other linguists, including Chomsky himself, have come to assign a larger role to semantics and lexical items. Nevertheless, they still assume that expression generation and comprehension are rule-governed, not produced by generalizations from past experience.

Natural languages also utilize *transformational rules*, that shift structures about in a sentence. The passive transformation in English is a good example. It does not expand a string of symbols, it shifts components around.

Linguists believe that all natural languages are special cases of a *universal grammar*, a species-general set of genetically determined rules that describe the rules that are allowed to exist in a specific language. Language learning, therefore, is not a process of generalizing from examples. Instead, a child learns by observing the language of his or her culture and matching these observations to the rules that would be permitted by the universal grammar. This is called *setting parameters*. Of course, there is no claim that this is a conscious process. What is claimed is that it is an inborn, genetically determined process that is different from general learning mechanisms.

The statements in the précis can only hint at the subtleties and complexities of modern linguistic theory. In the full text, Chapter 7/2LinguisticApproaches *provides an elementary discussion with examples. For still further analyses, readers may consult a modern linguistics text.*

7.3 Psycholinguistic Approaches

Psycholinguistic approaches to language deal with how language is produced and comprehended, rather than how language is to be described. Therefore, attention is shifted from language competence, where the goal is to determine the rules that generate well-formed expressions, to language performance, where the goal is to determine how the mind–brain system deals with language.

One of the most hotly debated issues is whether language is a special facility, with its own rules for learning and use, or a facility that has been produced by general mechanisms for learning, comprehension, and the control of attention. For instance, the idea that a universal grammar exists, and that learning a language amount to setting parameters in that grammar, is an extreme argument for a special facility. It is not clear to what extent the idea of a universal grammar can be tested empirically. However, we can test the idea that there are areas of the brain that appear to be specialized for language comprehension and use.

It has been evident since the 19th century that the brain contains special modules for language analysis. Early evidence was based on neuropsychological observations. People who suffer damage to Broca's area, in the left posterior frontal lobe, show deficiencies in syntactic processes. People who suffer damage to Wernicke's area are able to process sentences syntactically, but produce only meaningless strings of words. Conclusions that there are separate areas of syntactical analysis, semantic analysis, and thought have been confirmed by neural imaging studies. Furthermore, electrophysiological studies show that the brain makes different electrical responses to syntactic and semantic anomalies.

It is less clear how the modules interact. Do they process information independently, and then deliver the results to each other, or does the processing in one module have an influence on the others prior to its completion? To answer this question we turn to behavioral, rather than neuropsychological, research. Two broad classes of techniques have been used. One relies on the concept of diversion of attention. The idea is that if a person's attention is engaged in analyzing an expression, then a stimulus that arrives during the analysis should not be noticed until after the analysis is completed. For example, if a person is reading the sentence *The man who shot Mr. Ford feared Frank James*, and a click arrives as *Mr.* is presented, the click should be heard as arriving after *Ford*. Therefore, click migration from its usual place can be used to identify the units of psychological analysis. The second technique used is to observe eye movements during reading, based on the assumption that pauses and retracing indicate the course of sentence analysis.

These techniques have shown that clauses are both psychological and linguistic units of analysis. In addition, they have shown that people guess about the likely course of an analysis before the analysis is complete. As a result we can be surprised by "garden path" sentences such as *The horse raced past the garden fell*, because horse is initially assumed to be the subject of *raced*, forcing reanalysis of the sentence when *fell* is encountered.

Experiments on sentence comprehension are used to address two questions. Most obviously, they are used to reveal the algorithms that people use as they parse sentences. Although the evidence is mixed, the weight of the experimental results suggest that the syntactical and semantic modules interact, rather than simply pass information to each other. In addition, sentence processing can be compared across languages. It appears that different languages present substantially different computational challenges to the mind–brain system.

We now consider the question of whether language processing uses the same brain mechanisms that are used by other cognitive processes. Language analysis requires short term memory, but is it the same short term memory used by other cognitive acts? The evidence is mixed. Behavioral studies show that sentence comprehension becomes difficult when a person tries to understand sentences when simultaneously holding information in short term memory. For example, imagine that someone tells you his telephone number, and then continues to talk. The task of remembering the telephone number can interfere with language comprehension, and vice versa. This suggests that language comprehension uses the same short term memory used by other cognitive tasks. Alternately, there are neuropsychological reports of patients who have lost the ability to do short term memory tasks but can still comprehend speech.

Questions about the extent to which there are interactions between syntactical, semantic, and general cognitive processes can also be investigated by studying ambiguity resolution. Sentences such as *The spy slipped her insinuations into the conversation*, and *The spy slipped the documents under her slip* use different meanings of *slip* at different times. This illustrates lexical ambiguity. Syntactic ambiguities can occur, as in *She saw Ellen flying to California*, compared with *She saw the Grand Canyon flying to California*. Evidence suggests that when an ambiguity is encountered, several interpretations are considered unconsciously, in parallel, followed by selection of the interpretation that is correct in context. However, there is also some evidence that this depends on the individual. It may be that only people with high verbal processing skills consider multiple meanings. In addition, nonlinguistic analyses of a situation can bias the selection process, indicating further interactions between linguistic and more general cognitive processes.

LANGUAGE AND THOUGHT

Models of language comprehension proposed in the 1960–1970 era stressed the evidence for distinct syntactical, semantic, and pragmatic analyses. Although no single empirical demonstration of interactions between linguistic and nonlinguistic processing ruled out these models, the sum of the evidence made an approach based on assumptions about distinct processing models less and less attractive. As a result, there has been a shift toward models in which comprehension is guided by the constraints imposed by the lexical elements contained in a sentence. Verbs become particularly important, because they impose case-based constraints on many other elements in an expression. Just knowing that X admired Y tells us that X is an animate being, very probably, a human. Constraint-based analyses let us distinguish between *She saw Ellen flying to California* and *She saw the Grand Canyon flying to California*, for *the Grand Canyon* is not a semantically plausible subject of *flying*. In such models, expression comprehension is no longer a process of determining how an expression was generated, it is a process of assembly. Connectionist models similar to those described in chap. 4 have been developed to simulate some of the assembly processes. This approach represents a major challenge to the generative grammar approach, for it amounts to a claim that although the rules of a generative grammar may be a succinct description of a language, they do not have psychological reality. The debate is not over, but the success of modern connectionist studies of linguistic phenomena certainly suggests that the destruction of associationist approaches to language during the cognitive revolution of the 1950–1960 period was not as complete as has been claimed.

See Chapter 7/3Psycholinguistics *for amplification upon these ideas.*

7.4 Understanding Texts and Discourses

People do not speak or write in isolated expressions. We express ideas in coherent strings of expressions, or *discourses*. Discourses may be on such varied topics as baseball, novels, political speeches, and scientific articles. Can we find structures in discourse that are reflected in our memory and comprehension of a text or speech?

During the 1970s, attempts were made to develop generative grammars for discourses that were analogous to grammars for expressions. Grammatical analysis works moderately well for simple discourses, such as children's stories, but breaks down when applied to more complicated text. In fact, the analogy between formal languages and a language of discourse can be questioned on two grounds. The notion of a well-formed expression is reasonably clear, but the notion of a well-formed discourse is not. Also, a language, as defined in generative grammar, is the (infinite) set of well formed expressions constructed by applying grammatical rules to choose elements from a finite set of terminal lexical elements, words, and their inflections. The terminal element of a discourse is the proposition, and the set of propositions is infinite.

Nevertheless, discourses certainly do have structure. It has been claimed that discourses are built around schematic frames, such as the compulsory and explicit order of presentation of arguments in scientific journal articles. But if this were true, how would a reader–listener ever comprehend a discourse without first acquiring the schema? For these reasons the modern approach to discourse comprehension is to assume that comprehension is constructed, based on the assembly of commonly accepted, recognizable substructures. To illustrate, although a novel may have an unpredictable structure, the sequences within a novel, such as a visit to a physician, riding on an airplane, or having dinner, all have structures that are well known to the reader. Indeed, comedy writers from Shakespeare to modern day screenwriters have used confusions of these structures as a recurring theme. A senator (or other important figure) mistaken for a deliveryman is guaranteed to draw laughs.

These considerations leave us in something of a conundrum. On one hand, understanding a text or discourse must depend on understanding the expressions in it. On the other hand, it appears that you cannot understand a text unless you know what it is about. How does a reader know what the text is about before he or she understands it? Walter Kintsch, a professor at the University of Colorado, has addressed this problem by describing discourse comprehension as an interaction between bottom-up influences based on the recognition of propositions in the text, and top-down influences based on world knowledge. According to Kintsch's *construction-integration* model (1998), text comprehension requires readers to develop two models. The *textbase model* identifies important propositions in the text and relates them to each other. The *situation model* combines information in the textbase model with relevant information about the world. Kintsch's and similar models have provided frames for much of the current research on text comprehension. This approach emphasizes the constructive nature of text comprehension, as opposed to the emphasis on idea, then generation that was inherent in the story grammar approach.

Construction and integration works best when pieces of information are introduced in a way that makes it clear how they fit into both the textbase and situation models. Studies of comprehension show that there are a number of effective ways of doing this. One example is *first mention*, comprehension is easier to achieve when the first mentioned topic is the topic of the discourse. Another is *anaphoric reference*, tying different propositions together by using a general word or pronoun to refer to a topic mentioned earlier. These are only two of several techniques for producing a discourse that make up the recipient's construction-integration task. The study of different techniques may someday lead to a psychological basis for instruction in writing.

Understanding a text often requires inferences that go beyond the information in the actual text. If we read *Aloysius did not care that the dinner cost $150. Heloise had agreed to go out with him!* most of us will infer that Aloysius wished to make a good impression on Heloise. More generally, very few discourses explicitly impart all the information that the speaker wants the comprehender to have. Sometimes inferences are required to make sense of the textbase. The only way to connect the two sentences in the *Aloysius* vignette is to make the bridging inference described earlier. Other inferences are made, depending on the goals of the comprehender. Consider how the statement *Spike, the ace pitcher for the Mudhens, reported that he was unable to move his arm outward. He had been injured in an automobile accident in which he was struck from behind while stopped at a red light,* could be interpreted differently by different people. The Mudhen coach might draw the inference that someone would have to replace Spike in the game, the team physician might infer that there is damage to a tendon in Spike's shoulder, and Spike's lawyer might infer that damages were due. Theories of discourse comprehension distinguish between compulsory inferences, which must be drawn to tie a textbase together, automatic inferences, that depend only on highly overlearned common knowledge, and optional inferences that may be made or not, depending on the comprehender's purpose in examining a discourse.

For an expansion on these ideas with more detailed examples, see Chapter 7/4DiscourseComprehension.

7.5 Is There One Language of Thought?

Many linguists and psycholinguists write as if there is a single language of thought, or, *mentalese,* that is used to form ideas. External speech and writing simply express the real idea, the propositions in the mentalese statement. This idea has been challenged in two ways.

The first challenge to the concept of mentalese is the *dual-coding hypothesis*. According to this hypothesis, thoughts may be held in the mind in either a propositional form, or a spatial-visual form, as images that can be used in reasoning. The details of image-based reasoning were presented in chap. 6. I mention these again largely to remind the reader that thought may not be completely oriented toward verbal expression.

The second challenge to mentalese is an argument that has come to be known as the Sapir-Whorf, or Whorfian hypothesis. The Whorfian hypothesis states that thinking takes place internally, in the speaker's native language. Therefore, if two languages differ in the ease with which a particular thought can be expressed, two otherwise-equally competent persons, one speaking one language and one another, will differ in their ability to deal with the content of the thought. This is a flat-out challenge to the idea that a linguistic module computes the external expression of a thought (or analyzes an incoming external expression) but does not influence formation of the thought.

The Whorfian hypothesis has proven to be extremely difficult to test for a variety of reasons. One reason is that languages have relatively equal expressive power; anything that can be said in one language can be said, albeit perhaps in a clumsy manner, in another. However, two effects do seem to be well established. The first is that if language is used to code an experience, the way in which the language allows coding will influence memory for the experience. To illustrate, different languages break up the continuous color spectrum in somewhat different ways. This apparently influences a person's memory for the color of an object, but does not influence the person's perception of an object when it is present.

A similar effect has been shown for selective attention and semantic memory. Different languages direct our attention to different aspects of the world. For example, certain languages around the Pacific Rim have syntactic forms that require a speaker to attend to the shape of objects. Correlations have been shown between similarity ratings of objects and the different classification procedures used by a speaker's language.

For further discussion of the relation between thought and language, see **Chapter 7/5Language&Thought.**

A summary statement concerning language is contained in **Chapter 7/6Summary.**

8

The Organization of Knowledge

8.1 Introduction

One of the most powerful aspects of human thought is our ability to sort objects and experiences into categories and then apply our knowledge about the category to deal with the case at hand. This is an extremely handy thing to be able to do. Categorical reasoning is the basis of our legal system. The same sort of reasoning guides a physician when he makes a diagnosis.

A psychological theory of categorical reasoning has to address three questions: how categories are represented in the mind, how we come to form categories, given that all our experience is with instances of categories, and what rules of logic apply when we reason categorically. Ideally, we should like to answer these questions by observing people as they acquire and use categorical rules that are important to their everyday life. Category formation in young children is of special interest, because the basic concepts humans use in reasoning are acquired quite early in life. In practice, direct observation is seldom practical. Therefore, psychologists have resorted to two alternative strategies to study categorical reasoning. One is to examine the concepts that people have developed at particular points in the life span. For instance, a child's concept of animal can be related to an adult's, and a medical student's concept of a disease can be related to the concept held by a specialist with years of experience. The other strategy is to create a temporary learning experience within a laboratory environment to study how people come to develop categorization rules in this limited situation. For instance, an experimenter can create an artificial category of geometric objects (e.g., large black triangles), show participants examples and nonexamples of the category, and determine the conditions under which participants are able to identify the categorization rule.

These two ways of studying category learning have complementary strengths and weaknesses. Direct examination has ecological validity, but is limited by our ability to observe and control important aspects of the learning situation. Laboratory studies permit control, but the link between laboratory results and field situations is weak. Relatively little investigation of this link has been done, leaving it one of the major unresolved issues in cognitive psychology.

In most cases we shall consider, categorization is based on an analysis of the features of the object to be categorized. A feature is a *defining feature* if it is involved in the conceptual definition of a class. To use a category that will be the basis of a running example, the conceptual class of BEARS is defined genetically. All BEARS share common DNA sequences. A *characteristic feature* is an easily observable feature that is statistically associated with class membership. Size, dark fur, and an omnivorous diet are characteristic features of bears. Of course, a given feature may be both defining and characteristic.

The distinction between defining and characteristic features becomes important when we consider different mental representations of concepts. The *defining properties* point of view is that class membership is determined by a Boolean proposition over the range of defining properties. Therefore, a triangle is a right triangle if, and only if, one of its angles is a right angle, and a person is a citizen of the United States if (a) at least one of the person's parents was a U.S. citizen, or (b) the person was born in the U.S., or (c) the person has been granted citizenship by naturalization. The defining properties view is combined with a strong rule of inference. Every object in a class inherits all properties necessarily associated with class members.

Although the defining properties view is certainly used at some times, many of our everyday concepts seem to be based on graded *family resemblance*. Although the biologist may define BEARS genetically, for most people they are simply big, furry, fierce animals with short tails. Therefore, membership in a category is not a yes–no proposition, as it is in the defining properties view. Biologists, who use the defining properties approach, see robins, ostriches, and penguins as BIRDS. Psychologically, though, for many of us the robin is a very good BIRD, while ostriches and penguins are poor examples of BIRDS.

Family resemblance rules for class membership are often defined in terms of statistical associations between class membership and possession of characteristic features of the class. For instance, having fur is a typical, although not defining, characteristic of MAMMALS. More formally, letting Pr stand for probability, Pr(fur I MAMMAL) is high, although some mammals (cetaceans, humans, and a few other cases) do not have fur. In addition, some allowance has to be made for the perceptual salience of a feature. BEARS have shorter tails than most animals, but their short tails are not obvious, so size and shape make better characteristic features. Graded resemblance is closely linked to the concept of similarity, either between an object and some ideal description of a class member, or similarity between two objects in the same class.

Some categories refer to objects linked by a common theme. Examples are the Twelve Apostles and members of the United States Senate. *Goal-directed* categories are an important subset of thematic categories. The objects in a goal-directed category are linked by some desired end. Examples are the category of Things to be Removed When a Fire Breaks Out, or, Things to Bring on a Picnic. People are surprisingly good at inventing and using such categories as the need arises. In fact, we are so good at doing so, that some psychologists suggest that virtually all categories are made up on the spot, rather than representing ideas that were formed before they were needed.

Rules of inference permit us to reason about categories, cross categories, and specific instances within a category. A common principle is *reasoning by inheritance*; any subset of a category inherits properties of the more general category. The specific rules for inheritance depend on the type of category that we are dealing with. When a category is defined by logical propositions these propositions must apply to all members. Thus, the class REPUBLICAN WOMAN PRESIDENTIAL CANDIDATE is clearly defined, and the properties of an example known, even though (as of 2001) this particular concept has no exemplars.

The inheritance problem is more complicated when we deal with classes that are defined either by probabilistic rules or by similarities. When class definitions are truly probabilistic, as in the example of A DAY PRIOR TO A RAINSTORM, then the calculus of probabilities can be substituted for the rules of logical inference. One of the clearest examples of this is automated medical diagnosis, in which the probability of a disease is calculated given the results of diagnostic tests. Categories based on family resemblance pose more of a challenge, for the inference rules are not clear. Depending on the context, a DUCK can be considered a good or a bad BIRD. A good deal of psychological research has been directed toward finding the rules of inference that are used with family resemblance categories. Some progress has been made, but the issue is certainly not yet closed.

The distinction between early and late computation can be applied to categorical reasoning. A concept is established by early computation if learners develop their mental representation of a concept prior to having to use it. Concepts are established by late computation if a person invents categorization rules to solve a specific problem. Of course, the two types of categorical reasoning are not exclusive, for it could be that some category rules are established by early and some by late computation. The psychologist's dilemma is to determine which types of rules are susceptible to which types of computation.

There has been an ongoing debate about whether classes exist in the world, and hence, are discovered by people, or whether classes are constructs created by people to simplify reasoning about the world. Within this debate, there is also debate over the extent to which we are genetically wired to learn certain classes, especially during language learning, or whether the classes that we learn are a result of our particular cultural experiences.

There is agreement on one thing; concepts ought to group similar objects together. But what do we mean by similar? Many psychologists have adopted a geometric model, in which dimensions of variation are equated with geometric dimensions in a *semantic space*. In a semantic space model objects are represented as points in a metric space, the similarity of one object to another is determined by the distance between the points that represent them, and classes are associated with regions of the description space. To imagine how this might work, think of how athletes might be described by height and weight, and the difference between "football player space" and "basketball player space."

The *feature-based* view is a generalization of the dimensional view. According to it, objects are described by sets of features, whose values are not necessarily ordered. For example, one could regard religious behavior as a feature of a politician, and say that two individuals displayed similar religious behavior, without establishing an ordering of different religions. Similarity is increased when objects share features. Philosophers have objected to this approach on the grounds that any two objects share an infinite number of features. (For instance, every human being has the feature "has never been to Mars.") Psychologists can avoid the logical problem by pointing out that we deal with perceived similarities defined over a manageable number of attributes.

Finally, similarity can be based on shared structure (i.e., relations between primitive features, rather than on shared features). Many perceptual classifications, such as the concept of symmetry, appear to be of this nature.

It is easy to demonstrate that people do not simply try out different possible concepts until they find a useful organization of the world. Our experience underdetermines categorization rules, for experience does not rule out many possible categorizations that we never consider. Insofar as we know all green objects may actually consist of two classes, objects that are green now and will continue to be, and objects that will turn from green to red in the year 3000. Less bizarre examples can also be found, especially in the acquisition of a first language. Suppose a four-year-old who knows the meaning of the word cow sees a cow and a horse, and hears an adult say "horse." The child will quickly learn that the word horse refers to the new animal, although there is nothing in the child's experience to rule out the possibility that "horse" is simply an alternative name for cow. The child language learner assumes that new words are introduced for new objects.

If our experience underdetermines our concepts, how is it that people with similar experiences exhibit similar conceptual organization? The *nativist* argument is that we are genetically programmed to learn some concepts and not others. Concepts relating to language structure and concepts associated with natural kinds, such as the distinction between living and nonliving beings, seem to be part of our genetic heritage. An alternative explanation of communalities in conceptual organization is that the concepts themselves are not genetically determined, but that the algorithms we use to process information are. If this is true, two different people faced with the same insufficient evidence for a particular organization would select the same unproven conclusions. The two hypotheses are not inconsistent, for we may acquire some concepts through genetically determined preferences for a particular categorization and others through genetically or culturally determined biases to evaluate evidence in a certain way. Chapters 8 and 9 develop these topics in some detail.

A more detailed overview of issues can be found in Chapter 8/1Overview.

8.2 Models of Knowledge Organization Based on Analogies Between Similarity and Proximity

8.2.1–8.2.2 Spatial Models for Organizing Information: Basic Concepts

The basic idea of spatial mental models is that objects can be located on conceptual dimensions in a manner analogous to locating them on physical dimensions. Just as Paris is North and West of Rome on the East–West and North–South dimensions, perhaps (mentally) the concept WOLF is larger and fiercer than DOG on the dimensions of size and domesticity. Of course, no one believes that there is literally a mental space inside the head. The issue is whether the analogy to spatial layouts produces a useful information processing model of categorical reasoning. To answer this, we have to think carefully about what we mean by a spatial representation of information.

To facilitate our thinking, let us examine the ubiquitous graphs used to represent statistical information. Spatial relations on the graph represent conceptual information about the objects being displayed. For instance, arguments about global warming are frequently accompanied by graphs showing mean global temperatures over the past century or two. We are invited to make an inference about the time–temperature relation by observing the general direction of a line of temperature readings, taken over time.

In order to use such a graph we have to have a *memorization* operation that maps from attributes of the objects to dimensions on the graph, and a *retrieval* operation in which information is read off the graph. The memorization operation, called *scaling*, has been the topic of considerable discussion. The retrieval operation for a graph is visual perception. A good graph is one in which the crucial relationships are easy to read. Therefore, it is often useful to consider carefully how scaling should be done to facilitate reading.

The same idea applies when we use spatial models to represent a person's knowledge organization. Psychological similarity between objects is to be represented by distance in a hypothetical semantic space. Categories of similar objects should be defined by spatial proximity. For instance, in the space representing BIRDS, the hawk and the eagle (both raptors) should be plotted close to each other, and the robin and the thrush (both songbirds) should be close to each other and distant from the raptors.

The problem is that we do not know, in advance, what the dimensions of the mental space are. If we were dealing with height and weight, we can simply make measurements. Comparing two people in terms of, say, their suitability as political candidates, can be more complicated. However, it can be done. We now explore some of the methods used to make such comparisons.

The précis section barely touches on complex problems concerning scaling and weighting of measurements. For a more extended discussion of these topics, see Chapter 8/2SpatialModels/1-2BasicConcepts.

8.2.3 Constructing a Spatial Model of Knowledge Organization

Suppose that we had a set A = {a,b,c,d...} of objects, defined by their value on just one observable attribute. We further suppose that the attribute is measured on at least a linear scale. (*Scale types are defined in Chapter 8/2SpatialModels/1-2BasicConcepts.*) The example given in the main text is a set of squares, varying in the length of side (and hence, area). Other examples might be weights of varying sizes and lengths of lines. What sort of (one-dimensional) mental space represents the way we think about such objects?

The *psychophysical* approach to this problem is to find a function that maps the objectively measured weight into a corresponding psychological dimension, such as the relation between weight and perceived heaviness. This relation is called a *psychophysical function*. The function we use to illustrate the approach is *Stevens' law*, $x = y$, where x is the perceived (psychological) dimension, y is the measured physical dimension, is a scaling constant, and is a parameter whose value depends on the physical attribute being measured. More generally, if $f(y)$ is the psychophysical function being used to map from y to x, then the a th object has measurable value y_a and position $x_a = f(y_a)$ on the psychological scale.

The accuracy of the psychological scale can be evaluated by examining similarity ratings. These ratings can take a variety of forms, ranging from asking a person to rate the similarity of stimulus a to stimulus b to estimating the probability that observers will confuse stimulus a with stimulus b. The way accuracy is checked is to see if the perceived similarities between stimulus pairs (a,b) conform to the distance $|x_a - x_b|$ between the corresponding values (x_a, x_b) on the psychological scale. Let us put this more formally, as described next.

Let S_{ab} be the observed similarity rating between stimulus a and b. Presumably, this is a reflection of some *internal* "feeling of similarity," S_{ab} that is ordinally related to the observed measure. That is, regardless of the exact form of the similarity measure it should be the case that $S_{ab} \geq S_{bc}$ if and only if $S_{ab} \geq S_{bc}$. (In a concrete case, suppose that we determine the probability of calling an item 'a' when it is actually 'b.' Write this Pr(a|b). Pr(a|b) should be a monotonically increasing function of S_{ab}.) If judgments of similarity are made by determining distances between object positions in a semantic space, then S_{ab} should be a monotonically decreasing function of $|x_a - x_b|$. Because the observed similarity ratings are positive monotonic functions of internal similarity, $S_{ab} \geq S_{cd}$ if and only if $|x_a - x_b| \leq |x_c - x_d|$. The similarity data are observables, while the positions on the internal mental scale, the numbers $\{x_a\}$ are theoretical quantities derived without consideration of the similarity measures. Therefore, the theoretical operations can be evaluated by comparing the observed similarities to the ones predicted by the psychophysical model.

This argument is turned around in the *similarities based approach* to constructing a mental space. This approach reduces to assigning numbers for x_a, x_b and so forth, so that the distances conform to the observed similarities. That is, if possible, the theoretical numbers $\{x_a\}$ are selected, so that $|x_a - x_b| \leq |x_c - x_d|$ if and only if $S_{ab} \geq S_{cd}$. Therefore, the similarities cannot be used to test the model because they were used to construct it. On the other hand, the scale values of the attributes, the $\{y_a\}$ were not used to construct the mental space. Therefore, a psychophysical law, $x = f(y)$ can be discovered by the similarities based approach, whereas it is asserted in the psychophysical approach.

In many cases, the similarities approach is straightforward. Weight maps into perceived heaviness, light intensity into brightness, and sound pressure level into loudness. However, there are interesting cases in which it is not possible to assign stimuli to points on a single dimension and still satisfy similarity ratings. The best known example is color, a case discussed by Isaac Newton. Colors are measured by the wavelength of light. However, the psychological reactions (hues) associated with the shortest and longest wavelengths (the infra-red and ultra-violet hues) are perceived as similar. This shows that light, a one-dimensional physical stimulus, maps into a two-dimensional psychological color space.

We next move to situations in which the objects being compared vary on one or more known dimensions that are again measured on a linear scale. Think, for instance, of people who varied in height, weight, and age. It would make sense to judge similarity of appearance in this case. If a mental space approach is taken to modeling knowledge, the cognitive psychologist's problem is to understand the relation between the observable attribute space, Y, and the mental space, X, built on transformations of objects. Both the psychophysical and similarities based approaches can be applied.

The psychophysical approach is to map each attribute into a separate psychological dimension, and then locate the objects in the resulting space. Mathematically, objects $a, b, \ldots$ and so forth are now describable by vectors of attribute values. Thus, stimulus a would be described by $y_a = (y_{a1}, y_{a2} \ldots y_{aN})$ where N is the number of attributes. The problem is to map these vectors into vectors in a mental space, $x_a = (x_{a1}, x_{a2} \ldots x_{aN})$. When this is done, stimuli a, b, will be positioned at points x_a, x_b in the mental space X. Perceived (and observable) similarity judgments, the data set $\{S_{ab}\}$ should decrease as the distance d_{ab} between points x_a and x_b increases.

To illustrate, suppose that we mechanically applied Stevens' law to judgments of height and weight. We might first conduct studies of the perceived magnitude of stimuli that varied only in height and only in weight, to determine the Stevens' law parameters for height and weight. If we then have to deal with stimuli varying in both height and weight, positions in the mental space for any object, a, would be determined by

$$x_{a, height} = (height) y_{a, height}^{(height)} ; x_{a, weight} = \alpha(weight) y_{a, weight}^{(weight)}$$

where α(height), α(weight) *(height)*, and *(weight)* are the scale and growth parameters relating measured to perceived height and weight. Similarity measures could be related to distances in the resulting mental (X) space.

This approach has to be extended to deal with two complicating factors. The first is the problem of scales. The parameters establish the scale unit of the mental space. In the two-dimensional case each α parameter has to bear some sensible relation to the other α parameters, because the distance computation depends on the scale values of the individual dimensions. The problem is analogous to the problem of weighting scales when points are plotted on a two-dimensional scatter plot, as discussed in section 8.1 of the main text.

The second complicating factor is the computation of distance. In some situations, the psychological distance between multiattribute objects appears to be a (weighted) sum of the psychological distance between them on each attribute, separately. For instance, when asked to judge rectangles people probably judge height and width separately. In such cases the two attributes are said to be *separable*. In other cases, such as judgments of lights varying in wavelength and saturation, more holistic judgments seem to be the case. The attributes are said to be *integral*.

These distinctions are reflected in the algorithm used to compute distances. In the case of separable attributes, distance can be computed as the sum of distances along each psychological dimension,

$$d_{ab} = \Sigma_{i=1,N} | x_{ai} - x_{bi} |.$$

In the case of integral stimuli similarity judgments are best modeled by the familiar Pythagorean theorem,

$$d_{ab} = (\Sigma_{i=1,N} | x_{ai} - x_{bi} |^2)^{1/2}.$$

These two alternatives are often referred to as "city block" and Euclidean distance measures.

Neither the scale estimation or distance calculation problems are unsolvable, although they do complicate the psychophysical approach. As was the case in the one-dimensional situation, once the mental space has been constructed it can be evaluated by determining whether presumed distances between object locations are ordinally related to judgments of similarity between objects.

The similarity-based approach also applies to the case of multiattribute similarity judgments. Multidimensional scaling (MDS), a mathematical technique described in chap. 6, section 5, can be applied to position objects in a mental space in such a way that distances are inversely related to similarity judgments.

> *Mathematically inclined cognitive psychologists have devoted a great deal of effort to determining how one could develop a mental space based on judgments of similarity between multiattribute objects.* Chapter 8/2SpatialModels/3MentalSpaces *discusses both the one-dimensional and multidimensional case in depth. Several examples are offered. The discussion extends to the development of a universal law of generalization, a topic not covered in the brief analysis presented in the précis.*

8.2.4 The Multiplicative Similarity Model

Many laboratory studies of similarity and categorical reasoning have asked participants to rate the similarity of, or to learn a categorization for, objects that are composed by combining features of clearly defined attributes. Fig. 8.1 shows an example, cartoon birds that vary in wing shape, head shape, body color, and tail shape. The example is not hypothetical. There are dozens of categorization studies in the literature that use as stimuli birds, bugs, and mammals constructed in just this way. It has often been found that for this class of objects similarity judgments can be modeled by a special *multiplicative* model of similarity.

The idea behind the multiplicative model is that the similarities between objects can be determined by combining the similarities between the values of the objects on each of the attributes. In a concrete case, birds 1 and 2 in Fig. 8.1 have the same wing shapes and tail shapes but different head shapes and body colors. Birds 1 and 4 have the same head shape and body colors but different wing shapes and tail shapes. Is Bird 1 more like Bird 2 or Bird 4? The answer depends on how discrepant different wing shapes, tail shapes, head shapes, and body colors are seen to be, and how important each discrepancy is.

ORGANIZATION OF KNOWLEDGE 117

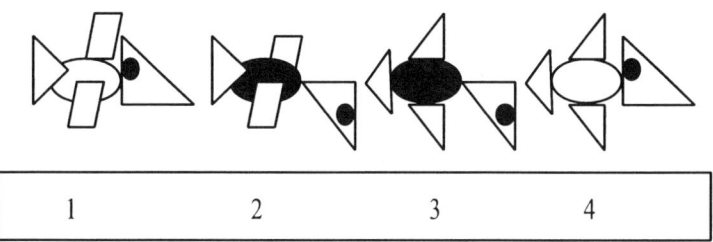

FIG. 8.1. Cartoon birds created by combining different wing shapes, tail shapes, head shapes, and body colors. (Only a few of the possible combinations are shown.) These "birds" are typical of the artificial birds, mammals, faces, and bugs that have been used to study how people judge similarity and learn categorization rules for arbitrary stimuli.

The multiplicative model presents a way of calculating overall similarity, based on attribute by attribute similarity. To explain it, one more bit of notation is needed. Assume that the stimuli are made up by choosing values on each of N attributes, and let y_{ai} be the value of object a on feature i. (For instance, if we replace a and i with bird numbers and descriptions, and suppose that body color is attribute 1, then y_{11} = white, y_{41} = black.) The similarity between two objects a and b on the ith attribute, considered alone, will be written $s(y_{ai}, y_{bi})$. We require that this be in the range $0 < s(y_{ai}, y_{bi}) \leq 1$, where 0 indicates an impossible state of infinite discrepancy, and 1 indicates perceived identity. The overall similarity between two objects is given by

$$S_{ab} = \Pi_{I=1,N}\, s(y_{ai}, y_{bi})^{w(i)},$$

where w(i) indicates the importance of the similarity comparison based on attribute i. Again taking a concrete case, if we were to compare birds 1 and 2, and assume that similarity is 1 if the attribute values are the same, 8-4 reduces to

$$S_{12} = \Pi 1^{w(tail)} s(black, white)^{w(body)} 1^{w(wing)} s(point\ forward, point\ down)^{w(head)}.$$

This model has been found to be widely applicable to studies in the literature that use artificial stimuli such as the birds of Fig. 8-1. Would it fit anywhere else? I offer one possible example, a contrast between automobiles that vary in body shape, body color, engine type, and so forth. Can the reader think of other examples? More to the point, can the reader think of the sorts of situations to which the model would or would not apply?

> Chapter 8/2SpatialModels/4MultiplicativeModel *develops the model in detail. The section contains more examples and develops the relation between the multiplicative model and spatial models of stimulus similarity.*

8.2.5 The Extension to Conceptual Objects

Thus far, we have been considering how to model perceived similarities between objects that differ along clearly defined attributes, such as the birds in Fig. 8.1. The concept of similarity applies more generally. It certainly makes sense to ask someone whether Germany resembles Sweden more than it resembles Japan, although it is not clear what attributes are being compared. Can we develop a *semantic space* to model the way people think about conceptual objects?

The psychophysical approach is of no use here, because we do not know what measurable attributes are involved in the comparison. The similarities based approach, and its computational implementation, Multidimensional Scaling (MDS), can be used because MDS begins with inter-object similarities and 'discovers' the mental space they imply, rather than going the other way around.

In one of the earliest applications of MDS, Henley (1969) asked college students to rate similarities between abstract animals (e.g., by asking which animal is more similar to LION, a WOLF or a ZEBRA). Multidimensional scaling showed that these ratings could be reasonably well modeled by a two-dimensional Euclidean space. Large animals were clustered at one end of one of the dimensions, and small animals at the other. The other dimension appeared to be a 'predacticity-domesticity' dimension. Reputedly fierce animals, such as the LION and WOLF appeared at one end, and the milder RABBIT and COW were positioned at the other. Intuitively, it certainly seems reasonable that animals are judged by size and ferocity. The important point, though, is that the MDS program discovered this relation on its own.

Since then, MDS has been applied to a very wide range of objects, both in cognitive psychology and in other fields. It has even had considerable impact on advertising, for marketing specialists sometimes ask potential customers to rate products, and then use MDS to determine the dimensions along which consumer products are perceived.

ORGANIZATION OF KNOWLEDGE

> *For a more extended discussion of the development of semantic spaces, see* Chapter 8/2SpatialModels/5Conceptual Objects.

8.2.6 Defining Classes in Spatial Models

If we are going to model mental representations of objects by points in a semantic space, it is logical to model mental representations of categories by regions within the same space. The result is a set of boundaries between classes, rather like the boundaries between countries on a conventional map. Expanding on the notion of animal spaces, this sort of logic produces BEAR country in one region of the space and DOG country in another.

This method of categorization has been called the *independent cues* model. The idea is that if a person encounters an unknown object the object's coordinates are determined along each semantic dimension, thus positioning the object in some region in semantic space. The object is then categorized as being a member of the class associated with that region of the space. The history of English common names for animals shows how this might work. The 17th and 18th century English explorers encountered animals that they had never seen at home. The North American *wapiti* (*cervus canadensis*) became an elk, and is to this day, because it looked like the Irish elk (*alces aslces*). At least the animals are related. In Australia, the (now extinct) thylacine (*thylacinus cynoephalus*) a marsupial predator, became the Tasmanian Wolf. According to the semantic space model, the explorers looked at the new animals, determined their locations in semantic space, and found that the point fell into regions associated with familiar European animals.

The problem with this model is that it is absolute; if object *a* falls into the region for class A, then object *a* must belong to class A. But it is easy to show that people often treat class membership as a graded category. American college students regard the ROBIN as a "better" bird than the PENGUIN. In fact the BAT, a mammal is given a nonzero rating as a BIRD. It is hard to believe that college students do not know that robins and penguins are both birds, or that bats are mammals. The difference is between the sort of spontaneous feeling that people have about class membership rather than the reasoning that they might do if they were answering questions in a zoology class.

The *prototype model*, an idea that can be traced back to Plato, has been proposed as a way of defining graded category membership within semantic spaces. Suppose that certain objects were designated as prototypical members of a class. New objects would be regarded as members of a class to the extent that their location in semantic space was close to the prototypes. For instance, college students in the United States seem to regard the robin as a prototypical bird. Other birds about the size of the robin, such as the thrushes and larger finches, are also good birds. The goose is not a good bird. Or at least, it is not a typical bird.

According to this logic the prototype is a point in semantic space, such as the centroid of the points of all class membership. Therefore, the prototype is an ideal, and need not correspond to an actual object. The class ROBIN appears to be prototypical of BIRDS because the descriptions of robins map to points in semantic space close to the prototype.

Both the independent features and prototype models are early computation models, because the categorization rule is defined before a person encounters the target object to be classified. The *exemplar model* for classification is a late computation model in which classes are defined at the time the target is encountered. According to the exemplar model classes are never explicitly defined. Instead, a person learns the semantic-space positions of specific objects that have been associated with class names. Thus a birdwatcher's semantic space would be littered, if you will, with memories of birds seen in the past. The target object (a new bird, in the birdwatching case) would be classified by mapping it into the semantic space and determining the class names associated with previously seen objects that were close by in semantic space.

The exemplar model has three major advantages over other models for category learning. It is simple, because it assumes that all a learner does is remember experiences. There is no need to perform any computations on the semantic space, such as positioning class boundaries or locating a prototype point. It is flexible, for the model can handle classifications that appear problematical from the viewpoint of other models. The GOOSE is very different from the ROBIN, but the GOOSE is quickly identified as a bird because it looks like other members of a subclass of BIRDS. The third, less obvious advantage is statistical efficiency. Nearest neighborhood classification is a surprisingly close approximation to maximum-likelihood classification. The chief disadvantage of the model is that it does not agree with the intuition that we do have some idea of the properties of abstract classes like BIRDS and WOLVES.

Chapter 8/2SpatialModels/6Classes *describes independent cues, prototype, and exemplar models in more detail. This section also contains a description of the experiments that are cited to support each model.*

8.2.7 Categorical Reasoning Based on Spatial Models

We now consider procedures for categorical inference based on semantic space models or, more generally, on the idea that category membership is a matter of degree. The inference procedures to be considered are also based on the idea that inferences are better treated as persuasive or nonpersuasive, rather than true or false.

The argument,

> Robins have mandibles
> Ostriches have mandibles
> Birds have mandibles

strikes most people as reasonable, even if we are not quite sure what mandibles are.[1] The argument,

> Penguins have sesamoid bones
> Auks have sesamoid bones
> Birds have sesamoid bones

is weak. Treating arguments as acceptable or not acceptable, to some degree, is consistent with regarding category membership as a matter of degree. What rule of inference do these examples illustrate?

Many people would justify accepting the first argument and rejecting the second on the grounds that if two such different birds as the ROBIN and the OSTRICH have a property, then it is a property of all birds. The PENGUIN and the AUK are unusual birds, and are similar to each other but different from most other birds. Therefore, they might well share a property that is lacking in more typical birds.

The *semantic coverage* model connects such intuitions to semantic space models of knowledge organization. The idea is that when a property is known about a particular object it is associated with the point representing that object in semantic space. When an assertion is made about a class of objects (as in, *birds have mandibles*), the assertion is accepted to the extent that the property in question has been associated with points widely distributed in the region belonging to the class. If an assertion is made about a specific object (as in *Albatrosses have sesamoid bones or sparrows have sesamoid bones*), a search is made about the point that the object (the ALBATROSS or the SPARROW) occupies in semantic space. The assertion is accepted to the extent that the property in question has been associated with points close to the target object's location. The semantic coverage model goes

---

[1] The mandibles are the upper and lower parts of the beak.

well beyond this informal presentation. The details are presented in the main text.

Fuzzy reasoning is a formal method of reasoning that was developed well before proposals for semantic space models (Zadeh, 1965), but that is certainly compatible with them. The driving intuition behind fuzzy reasoning is that in much of our everyday reasoning set membership is a matter of degree. To Americans, at least, HORSEMEAT is not usually considered a human food, while BEEFSTEAK is. However HORSEMEAT is served in certain locations and situations. According to fuzzy logic the degree of membership of BEEFSTEAK in the set FOOD is nearly 1.0, while HORSEMEAT is considerably lower but not at zero. More formally, if A is a fuzzy category and a an object, then the category membership of a is A, $c_A(a)$, ranges from 0 to 1, where 1 means "absolutely a member of the category" and 0 means "in no circumstances a member." All that is needed to connect this idea to semantic space models is to let c_A be some reasonable function of the semantic space properties of class A and object a, such as the distance between x_a and the location of the class prototype.

Fuzzy logic contains rules of inference for categorical reasoning that are analogous to the classic rules of the predicate calculus. For example, suppose that for some object, a, $c_A(a) = x$, where $0 \leq x \leq 1$. The extent to which object a is a member of the contrast class, ~A, is given by $c_{\sim A}(a) = 1-x$. Similar inference rules apply for set intersection, where $c_{A \cap B}(a) = \min(c_A(a), c_B(a))$, and union, $c_{A \cup B}(a) = \max(c_A(a), c_B(a))$ More complicated arguments can be built up from these basic rules.

Fuzzy set theory has enjoyed some success both in the popular press and in engineering applications, as an alternative to reasoning based on Boolean logic. It has had much less acceptance in cognitive psychology. One reason for this is that the function for assigning set membership must be at the core of any psychological theory of categorical inference. Fuzzy set theory only defines the range of the membership function. Another problem is that the inference rules in fuzzy set theory may lead to unacceptable conclusions. A baked apple may be an excellent BROWN APPLE without being a very good BROWN or a very good APPLE. This is contrary to fuzzy logic's rule for set intersection. For these reasons, fuzzy logic is probably not a very good psychological theory. However, it does point the way to the need for some sort of inference rules to augment semantic space models of category organization.

See Chapter 8/2SpatialModels/7InferenceSystems *for expansions on these models.*

8.2.8 Behavioral Violations of the Axioms of Spatial Models

Certain observations about the way people treat similarity appear to contradict basic notions of what a spatial model is. The first objection is that distances between two points (object representations) should remain constant across comparisons. In one often-cited study it was shown that, in the context of the 1970 cold war period, American students thought that AUSTRIA was most similar to SWEDEN in the comparison "Which country is most like AUSTRIA: SWEDEN, HUNGARY, POLAND." However, when the comparison of AUSTRIA was to SWEDEN, NORWAY, HUNGARY the students chose HUNGARY. In a semantic space model, this is equivalent to saying that the distance from AUSTRIA to SWEDEN is less than the distance from AUSTRIA to HUNGARY in the first comparison, but greater in the second. How can this be?

This finding is usually explained by saying that in the first comparison there is an implication that politics should be considered, because at the time Austria and Sweden were neutral in the East–West confrontation, while Poland and Hungary were members of the Warsaw Pact group. The second comparison implies that geography is important. A semantic space model can handle the results, by weighting each dimension in accordance with its importance in context. But then we have to explain how context is established.

Violations of symmetry are even more bothersome. In any spatial model, the distance from a to b is the same as the distance from b to a. The same is not true of ratings of similarity. North American students consistently rate NORTH KOREA as being similar to CHINA, but do not see CHINA as being similar to NORTH KOREA.

Findings like this have lead to the development of several alternative models of the organization about knowledge. We describe some in the next section.

For an expansion on the nature of the challenge to spatial modeling see Chapter 8/2SpatialModels/8Challenges.

8.3 Nonspatial Models

The *feature contrast model* developed by Amos Tversky and his colleagues is probably the leading challenger to semantic space models. In feature contrast theory objects are represented as bundles of features without any reference to a space. ROBIN, then, would be represented by a set of statements about what a person knows about ROBINS (medium size bird, brown with orange breast, sings, and so forth) rather than by a position in a space. Similarity comparisons are made by considering the extent to which the two objects share features and the extent to which one or the other of the two objects possesses unique features.

Tversky pointed out that the way that the comparison is stated will determine what sets of features are considered to be important. If a respondent is asked to say how different A is from B attention is focused on the unique features of A. If the question is about how similar they are, attention is focused on shared features. In addition, comparisons typically assign different roles to the A and B terms. If the question is "How similar is A to B" (at least according to Tversky) attention focuses on the extent to which the features of A are also features of B, and vice versa. In this case, asymmetry of comparison can be produced simply by different degrees of knowledge. Americans might see RUGBY as being similar to FOOTBALL because most of the (very few) things that they know about RUGBY (players tackle man with the ball, ball is carried over a line to score) are true of FOOTBALL, but that FOOTBALL is not similar to RUGBY because an American can think of many things about football (highly specialized positions, set plays, players virtually wear armor, coach controls game by sending in plays) that are not true of RUGBY. An Australian, with more knowledge of RUGBY than FOOTBALL, might see FOOTBALL as similar to RUGBY, and RUGBY different from FOOTBALL.

It was once thought that semantic space models had to be rejected in favor of feature contrast theory, or something like it, simply because of the observed asymmetries in "Is A like B" comparisons, and the sensitivity of comparisons to contexts, as in the case of the AUSTRIA comparisons just described above. This is not true, for certain special cases of feature contrast theory can be accommodated by an expanded spatial model. It is not clear whether the asymmetries and context sensitivities observed by Tversky and his colleagues satisfy the special case conditions.

So what are we to believe? Should we use feature contrast or semantic space models as ways of understanding knowledge organization? I suggest that this is the wrong question. Instead, we should try to determine the characteristics of situations in which each type of model provides a useful way of looking at a phenomenon of interest. More generally, both semantic space models and feature contrast models are ways of summarizing cognitive behaviors, not descriptive statements about what is going on inside the brain. Therefore, we should not ask '"Are they true?" Instead we should ask "Are they useful ways of understanding the problem at hand?"

> *Feature contrast theory is presented informally.* Chapter 8/3FeatureContrastTheory *provides a mathematical treatment both of the theory and its relation to semantic space models.*

8.4 Probabilistic Categorization

In some circumstances, class membership can only be known up to a probability. What, for instance, is the probability that tomorrow will fall into the class of things known as RAINY DAYS? There are two questions that can be asked about probabilistic categories; why use them at all, and if they are to be used, how do people estimate the probabilities involved?

Studies of naming provide insight into why categorical reasoning is useful. Any object can be described as being in many different classes. The thing that is supporting me as I write this text is alternatively, a swivel chair with adjustable height, a chair, a piece of furniture, and a thing that has never been to Mars. When I describe this object to another person, I want to send the shortest possible message that describes the object in sufficient detail so that the receiver of the message knows what I am talking about. "Bring the adjustable-height swivel chair over here" is too specific, "Bring the piece of furniture" is not specific enough.

People are remarkably efficient in their naming practices. They name things at a *basic level* category, such as CHAIR or CAT, that provides a surprisingly efficient coding of information. And as would be expected, if the context changes people's behavior changes. Dog show judges refer to COLLIES and GERMAN SHEPARDS, where most of us just say DOG.

To achieve optimally efficient categorization it is necessary to compute entropy measures for different levels of categories. (See the discussion of information processing theory, in chap. 2.) No one thinks that this is done explicitly. It turns out, though, that a well-known psychological phenomenon, *probability matching*, in which people learn the conditional probabilities of Pr('object a has property x' | 'object a is in class A') can approximate the calculation of entropy.

How do people estimate the probabilities involved? From a statistician's viewpoint, they do so rather badly. Two errors stand out. Laboratory studies have shown that people will confuse the typicality of an object as a member of a class with the probability that it is in the class. For instance, if a woman is described as being a politically active supporter of women's rights and exceptionally careful and precise in dealing with numbers some people will claim that she is more likely to be a FEMINIST AND AN ACCOUNTANT than to be a FEMINIST or an ACCOUNTANT, both unqualified. This violates the laws of probability, for Pr (A & B) $\leq$ Min(Pr(A), Pr(B)). In other cases, people ignore base rates, classifying an observation as likely to be a member of a class for which it seems typical, even if there are other, far more common, classes to which it could belong. The correct strategy is captured by the advice allegedly given to medical students; if you hear hoof beats, think horses, not zebras. Despite this advice, medical personnel have been shown to diagnose a case that is typical of a rare disease, but atypical although possible of a common disease, to be the rare disease even if the common disease is more likely.

Although studies on errors in probabilistic reasoning show that people do not make the probability estimates that statisticians would, it is reasonable to suppose that some sort of probability estimates are made. This assumption alone is sufficient to connect probabilistic models to semantic space models. In the *exemplar density* approach, it is assumed that a person represents his/her experience with particular exemplars of a class by a probability density function, centered over a particular point in semantic space. The difference between the exemplar density approach and the semantic space approach is that an object *a* is represented by a "smeared out" probability function centered on the point x_a in semantic space, rather than being represented by the point. Therefore, a new object *b* would be recognized as *a* if the probability density function for *a*, at point x_b in semantic space, were sufficiently high to warrant such identification.

The exemplar density model can be used to explain many of the behavioral phenomena that were used as evidence against semantic space models, including observations of asymmetry in comparing A to B or B to A. The reasons for this are not intuitively obvious, so one has to work out the mathematics. This is described in the main text.

More lengthy discussions of probabilistic models, including several examples, can be found in Chapter 8/4Probabilistic Models. *The discussion includes the mathematical argument for the exemplar density model.*

Chapter 8/5Summary *places the ideas presented in this chapter in a broader context, and points toward a further discussion of categorical reasoning in chap. 9.*

9

Categorical Reasoning Based on Conscious Strategies

9.1 Introduction

The models presented in chap. 8 are information processing level models. They are intended to apply to all cases of categorical reasoning, regardless of the topic. The mechanisms of reasoning (e.g., placing objects in semantic space and calculating distances between them) are assumed to be hidden from conscious inspection, although the similarity between objects that results from these calculations (e.g., a feeling) is conscious. This chapter considers situations in which the categorical reasoning process is explicit, and therefore, subject to conscious control.

A brief expansion on this paragraph is contained in Chapter 9/1Introduction.

9.2 Propositional Categories

Propositional categories are categories in which membership is determined by defining propositions. Some excellent examples are found in two quite different fields, law and mathematics. Laws specify the rights and obligations of certain categories of people, and proscribe specific categories of behavior. A CITIZEN OF THE UNITED STATES is a person who meets certain legal tests concerning birth or naturalization. In mathematics every RIGHT TRIANGLE has exactly one 90° angle. The rules of inference are simple. Any property that is true of a class is inherited by all its members. Intersections, subsets, and complementary sets are defined by the rules of the predicate calculus; essentially arguments based on statements like "For all X, proposition Y is true," and "For some X, proposition Y is true."

It has been claimed that propositional categories, and the inference rules related to them, are not psychological constructs because of the difficulty we have adequately defining virtually anything, and because of the variety of phenomena related to graded resemblance that were discussed in chap. 8. The position I take is that human categorical reasoning can proceed either on the basis of similarity, probability, or something like logical reasoning based on propositionally defined categories. When people reason propositionally, they are always aware of doing so; when they reason based on similarity or probability, they may be aware of what they are doing.

Saying that people can reason propositionally is not the same as saying that they are using a logician's rules of inference. By the standards of formal logic, people often make errors. Philip Johnson-Laird and his colleagues (1983) have studied this topic for more than 20 years and have developed a psychological model of the way in which people approach problems in categorical reasoning. Johnson-Laird argued that when people are asked to accept or reject a statement of the form *Premise: Conclusion* they attempt to imagine all different possible interpretations of the premises ('models,' to use Johnson-Laird's term), and ask whether the conclusion would be true in each interpretation. Errors occur if there are simply too many models to keep track of, thus overwhelming working memory.

Johnson-Laird's approach deals with how people use established propositional categories after they have been defined. There has also been considerable study of how people develop definitions of propositional categories, after having observed examples of things to which the category label either does or does not apply. In most of these studies an experimenter constructs a population of stimuli (e.g., geometric figures that can vary in shape, color, and size). Some subset of the features is then selected to be the defining features of a class. Continuing with geometric figures, the experimenter might decide that all large black figures are to be called GAX. The experimenter then shows the participant a number of examples of GAX and NOT GAX figures. The participant's task is to determine what rule the experimenter has selected.

Early research using this paradigm suggested that people act as statistical accumulators, simply noting correlations between the presence or absence of a feature and the use or nonuse of the class name. (In the example above there would be a correlation between the presence or absence of the features large and black and the use of the name GAX.) Subsequent research shows that this is not the case. Instead of being statistical counters, people appear to be active hypothesis developers.

Several different strategies of hypothesis development have been observed. One is to adopt the strategy that the necessary and defining features of a category are those that are shared by all known members of the category. This procedure, which is called *conservative focusing*, has been observed in some situations. However, another strategy is far commoner. People often simply guess (i.e., select one feature that is contained in the first example they are shown), and continue with this hypothesis until it leads to an error. Following the error they guess again, without much, if any, concern for their previous guesses. This may seem a surprisingly inefficient strategy. However a mathematical model, the *one-element model*, that assumes random guessing can be shown to be an extremely accurate predictor of behavior in rule-learning situations.

The situation becomes more complicated when the rule to be learned involves a disjunction, such as BLACK OR CIRCLE. (This is not an obscure rule. The category CITIZEN OF THE UNITED STATES is defined by a disjunctive rule.) Neither the conservative focusing strategy or the one element model applies. However, there are more complicated models that will work. They all make use of the fact that any categorizing rule can be stated as a sequential decision tree; first ask about Feature A, and then, depending on whether A is present or not, ask about Feature B or C. The process is continued until enough information has been accumulated to classify an item.

Psychological studies have shown that the complexity of the decision tree representing a categorizing rule is a fairly good indicator of the difficulty that people will have in learning that rule. Computer simulation programs have been written that can mimic the learning process. These programs have been combined with a variety of the one-element model, so that the resulting model is known as a *rule plus exception* model. The idea behind it is that learners seek simple rules to categorize objects, and are willing to memorize a list of exceptions. When the list of exceptions becomes too unwieldy, the learner seeks a second simple rule that applies to the exceptions.

We can summarize the laboratory studies on learning of propositionally defined categories by stating that people actively test hypotheses of what the answer is, but they are rather inefficient in generating the hypotheses to be tested.

> *For a more extended discussion of how people learn artificial categorization rules, see* Chapter 9/2Propositional Catgories. *This section explains conservative focusing, the mathematical basis of the one-element model, and sequential decision making procedures in more detail.*

9.3 Categorization Based on Knowledge

The experiments described thus far have all been based on what has been called the *standard model* for experiments on categorical reasoning. The standard model is based on three assumptions: that it is possible to classify an object given its description, that the rules uncovered in the experimental situation apply in all situations, and that the participant's reasoning is based on information presented by the experimenter, rather than information that the participant has acquired prior to entering the laboratory. The last assumption, which greatly increases the experimenter's control of the situation, is at the heart of the argument for studying the categorization of arbitrary objects such as geometric patterns, and for asking people to reason about obviously made-up worlds in which all chemists can be beekeepers if the experimenter says they are. (More formally, situations like this call for reasoning about *blank predicates*, statements that have no meaning outside of the laboratory.)

Philosophers have argued that the categories people make, spontaneously, carry with them the idea that each category has an essence, and that the an object remains in the category as long as it does not undergo some transformation that changes this essence. For instance, a lion remains a member of the category LION if its fur is shaved off. In some cases, the essence of a class is defined by the relationship that class members maintain with other class members, or with ideas that bind the class together. Membership in social groups, especially religious groups, illustrate this idea. The important thing is not that a person looks or acts in a certain way, but that they adhere to a consistent set of beliefs that then dictate their behavior.

It has been claimed that certain *natural kinds*, closely related to the idea of essence, are developed relatively early in life. The idea of a life-form is one of these. Returning to the example of a LION with its fur shaved off, four- and five-year-olds may maintain that the animal is transformed into something different if its appearance is changed. Ten-year-old children do not, but will accept the idea that a LION might be changed into a TIGER if a surgeon changed its insides. Similar developments of the idea that some transformations change the essence of an object while others do not have been observed in other fields. These include such abstract ideas as primitive counting (e.g., the concept of cardinality of a set of up to about five objects) and the notion that good or bad behavior depends on intent rather than outcome.

There has been considerable debate about the extent to which natural kinds are innate or are learned. The *behaviorist* position emphasizes learning, the *nativist* position emphasizes the notion of innate concepts. The evidence seems to lie inbetween behaviorism and nativism. Some concepts, including numerosity and various concepts about language, do seem to be innate. Other widespread ideas about essence and transformation seem to be the result of a general learning mechanism, interacting with a regular environment. A definitive list of the two types of concepts has yet to be developed.

Both the behaviorist and the nativist positions agree that classes exist because they are useful for thought. These uses fall under two broad categories. Sometimes knowledge about class properties is useful because it guides interactions with class members. This is particularly easy to see for socially defined classes. Once a person is identified as a class member, we know how to deal with them; one makes different requests of physicians and lawyers. At other times, knowledge of an object's class membership serves to highlight certain features that are an essential part of the object, although this essence may not be immediately obvious. We recognize that lions and tigers are cats because they represent a permissible transformation in size from a prototypical cat. An animal that is approximately the size of the prototypical cat, and that has long silky hair, as some cats do, but that barks (the PEKINGESE) is not a cat because barking and nonretractable claws are impermissible transformations from the prototype cat.

The interaction and essence view of concepts can be applied to the same objects, in different contexts. A study of college students' views of WATER illustrates this nicely. Chemically, something is WATER to the extent that it is pure H_2O. In the experiment, college students were asked to estimate the extent to which different types of liquids (e.g., SWAMP WATER, BROOK WATER) satisfied this essence view of WATER. Next, students were asked to rate similarities between different types of water. The students responded with an interactionist view, in which similarities were based on the way different types of WATER were used, rather than the extent to which the types had equal amounts of H_2O. The students believe that SWAMP WATER may be only 70% H_2O, but it is still WATER because it is a form of naturally occurring WATER that enters into understandable interactions with other objects. (BOTTLED WATER is an example of another subclass of WATER, that implies other interactions.) TEA, believed to be 90% H_2O, is not WATER because it fails a crucial test of interaction. An ordinary person can make TEA, but not WATER.

WATER is only one of the many classifications people use in which they mix the interaction and essence views of categorization. The main text describes some extended studies on classifications of animals by three different groups: zoologists, American university undergraduates, and members of the Itzaj Maya, a forest-dwelling Central American native group. The zoologists used an essence view of categories, based on a theory (genetics) of what it means for two animals to be related. The undergraduates approached this view, but on occasion, resorted to an interactionist view related to ecology. For instance, the undergraduates saw the COYOTE as more similar to the FOX than the DOG, whereas in fact, the COYOTE is virtually a breed of DOG and the FOX is a separate species. In terms of interactions, though, DOGS make good pets but COYOTES and FOXES do not. Ecological considerations were even more important to the Maya, who interact more extensively with animals. One of the most striking differences was the Maya's use of FOOD ANIMAL as a basis for rating similarity, a consideration that was not part of the zoological or undergraduate classification scheme.

Such findings are not confined to reasoning about animals. The same sort of reasoning has been illustrated in formal studies comparing botanists', landscape designers', and maintenance personnel's view of TREES. It seems quite likely that similar findings would be found in many areas of life.

In the experimenter's laboratory, a class exists because the experimenter says it does. Outside the laboratory, classes exist for a purpose. What a learner believes about this purpose can influence the sorts of categorization rules the learner considers. This has been shown by experiments in which people are presented with exactly the same set of objects, categorized in the same way, but given two different cover stories that explain why the categorization came to be. In one case, the cover story might suggest diagnosis; the participant is told that "Patients who have disease A display these symptoms." In another case, the cover story suggests causation, as in "People who display these symptoms cause emotional reaction A in other people." Although the formal statistics of the two situations are the same, college student participants developed different rules depending on the cover story. In the diagnostic situations, they looked for patterns of features that would indicate the disease; in the causal situation, they counted the number of features that might contribute to a reaction.

Similar behavior has been found in a more natural, but less controlled situation. College students were shown children's drawings of people. In one example, the pictures were divided into two groups that were labeled as having been drawn by different groups of children. In the other example, the pictures were said to have been drawn by normal or disturbed chil-

CATEGORICAL REASONING 133

dren. The students were asked to find details in the pictures that identified their source. When the sources were simply groups of children, the students developed categorization rules based on concrete features, such as observing that in one set of drawings people always had their arms at their sides. When the sources were said to be normal or disturbed children, much more complicated, abstract rules were given.

In each of these cases, the experimental participants were asked to find rules for exactly the same division of objects into classes, across conditions. Therefore, if learning proceeded by noting statistical associations between features and category names the same rules should have been produced, regardless of the cover story. This outcome is predicted by all associationist and abstract hypothesis testing models of rule-learning, including connectionist models and the tree-growing models described earlier. The cover story did make a difference in the rules that people developed. This shows that at the representational level, application of knowledge can override learning algorithms that are defined at the information processing level.

For further details on how knowledge can influence the way that categorization rules are learned and applied, see Chapter 9/3Knowledge.

9.4 Conceptual Coherence

Classes are useful to the extent that they group together similar objects, and put dissimilar objects outside the class. But what do we mean by similar? In chap. 8, we explored notions of similarity based on the possession of common features. Next, we examine a more intellectual concept of similarity.

Virtually all objects of thought have internal structures that relate elements to elements, and relations to relations. Two objects can be seen as similar because they have similar relational structures. By this criteria, tennis is similar to badminton and dissimilar to golf, because of similarities in the method of scoring and style of play. However, the same two objects may be embedded in different relations for different purposes. If we were discussing the role of money and financial sponsorships in sport, tennis and golf become similar, and badminton, still an amateur sport, is the odd game out.

Recent research has emphasized the fact that objects can only be compared (i.e., similarity in the sense discussed here is only defined) when the relational structures of objects can be aligned in some reasonable way.

When we are discussing the nature of the games, tennis and badminton are aligned, because the shuttle and the ball play similar roles, as do the nets, racquets, and scoring systems. Tennis and golf are much harder to align. When we discuss sport financing, though, the alignment between tennis and golf is almost perfect. Golf and tennis stars, hosts of anonymous "good players," tournaments, television, and sponsors stand in the same relation to each other in the two sports.

We conclude that at the representational level, where reasoning is conscious and overt, there is more to similarity than can be captured by notions like semantic spaces and feature bundles.

For an extended discussion of similarity based on analogous structures see Chapter 9/4ConceptualCoherence.

9.5 Relations Between Concepts

Concepts do not exist in isolation. We know that ROBINS are a subset of BIRDS, and that being BIRDS, they inherit the properties of birds. A theory of categorical reasoning has to explain how the mind deals with relations between concepts.

The *semantic network* model of conceptual relations pictures the mind as if it contained a network of nodes, representing categories, and arcs representing relations between categories. In semantic network theories, ROBIN is represented by a node. This node is connected to the node for BIRD by a subset–superset arc, and the node for BIRD is connected to FLIES by a property-of arc. Therefore, to answer the question "Can ROBINS fly?" the mind first activates the node for ROBIN, then for BIRD, and then for FLIES. Other questions can be answered by similar network searches.

If this model is realistic, computational activity in the network should predict indices of computational effort by the mind. To some extent they do. If we construct a reasonable network representation of what we think people know (e.g., that ROBINS are BIRDS and that BIRDS fly), the number of arcs between two concepts in the network is a rough predictor of the time it takes to answer a question about their relation. People are faster to answer questions like "Is a ROBIN a BIRD?" than, "Is a ROBIN an ANIMAL?" Other analogies between reaction times to questions and the computational effort required for an appropriate search of the network have also been noted. These results have made the notion of representing conceptual relations by semantic networks seem quite powerful.

Other behavioral observations show disparities between what people do and what we would expect them to do if the network model were correct. People are quick to reject a statement of set inclusion about items that are distant from each other in a network. The question "Is a ROBIN an AUTOMOBILE?" will be rejected more rapidly than "Is a ROBIN a HAWK?" A network search procedure would produce the opposite result, for an assertion could not be denied until both nodes were located and the relation between them determined. The time needed to do this would increase as the number of arcs between nodes increased. The fact that people are quick to reject statements associating distant objects with each other indicates either that the mind has a way of looking at the overall network, rather than searching it on a node-by-node basis, or that the network model is not an accurate picture of what the mind is doing.

A second problem with the network model is that it implies a reasonably permanent structure relating concepts to each other. Humans deal easily with conceptual relationships that are defined in context. A robin is a large bird in the company of sparrows, and a small one in the company of crows. It is not clear how a semantic network model can deal with context-dependent properties and classifications.

We conclude that semantic networks are useful for representing some relations between concepts, but fail to represent the flexibility that the mind has.

An alternative way to understand relations between concepts is to try to understand how concepts are changed as they are combined. Going back to an earlier example, a BROWN APPLE is well defined, although APPLES usually are not BROWN. What are the rules for forming and understanding compound categories? In chap. 8, it was noted that the fuzzy set intersection rule does not work. But what does?

It has been argued that concepts like BROWN APPLE or BEACH BICYCLE are "emergent," rather than being created by a mechanical combination of the properties of each concept. Unfortunately, it is not clear what emergent means. Two suggestions have been made. One is that the application of the modifying concept (BROWN in BROWN APPLE) changes a property of the base concept (APPLE), and when it does, forces a change in any other properties of the base concept that are in a structural relationship with the changed property. By this reasoning, once an APPLE is referred to as a BROWN APPLE its color is changed, and therefore, other properties are made consistent with BROWN. The apple becomes COOKED and SUGARED, neither a property of the normal APPLE.

A second way of defining emergent depends on an analogy between conceptual combination and the ideas of construction-integration theory, as applied in linguistics. Conceptual combinations create constraints on the base model, to the point that only one possible interpretation of the base model can work. This is why such disparate terms as MATHEMATICAL MODEL and FASHION MODEL are understandable.

Although these ideas may provide a start toward understanding how people relate concepts to each other, they are only a start. Understanding conceptual relations is one of the big issues confronting cognitive science.

For more on conceptual relationships, see Chapter 9/5ConceptualRelations.

A reprise of our knowledge of categorical reasoning can be found in Chapter 9/6Reprise.

10

Reasoning

10.1 The Relation Between Elementary and Complex Cognition

In this chapter, we discuss human reasoning and problem solving. The reason for not doing so earlier in the volume is that most cognitive psychologists believe that complicated reasoning, such as that displayed by lawyers, judges, and scientists can best be understood by reducing it to elementary actions of memory, perception, and knowledge organization. Therefore, it makes sense to look at these functions first, and then look at complex cognition. This opinion is not universally shared. Some psychologists argue that everyday reasoning is so complex that it can only be understood by studying it directly. This still permits laboratory research, but only when the behaviors being studied are very challenging. An example would be a study of how participants played a complex computer simulation of decision making, such as the decision making of an industrial plant manager. Another group of psychologists argue that everyday behavior is tightly constrained by the situation in which it occurs, including the social situation. According to this group, cognition is *situated* in the place it occurs. Therefore, school and workplace cognition should be studied in the field rather than the laboratory.

In general, this chapter follows the standard view that complicated cognition can be studied as an outgrowth of simpler mental processes.

For an expansion on this brief introduction, see Chapter 10/1Overview.

10.2 Deduction and Inference

Deductive problem solving begins with the statement of a situation and a set of rules of inferences. The rules of inference are then applied to determine if the original situation implies some desired situation. This is the formal view of problem solving in mathematics, especially algebra and geometry, and in symbolic logic. In each of these fields the original problem statement is translated into a symbolic form of the "givens" of the problem and a symbolic statement of the "to be proven" (goal) statement. Rules of inference based on the symbolic form are then applied to derive the symbolic form of the goal statement from the symbolic form of the initial statement. Techniques for achieving a solution of the symbolic problem are called *weak* problem solving methods, for they operate on the symbolic form of the statement, without any appeal to the meaning of the symbols in a world outside of logic or mathematics.

The opposite of a weak problem solving method is, naturally enough, a strong problem solving method. *Strong* methods take advantage of constraints in the particular situation. To see the difference between the two, we can contrast the way personal computer (PC) systems are assembled today to how they were assembled in the early 1980s. In modern systems the plugs and sockets for the computer, display device, keyboard, and other accessories all have different shapes. As a result, most consumers find that if they attach everything together in the only way physically possible the configuration is probably going to be correct. Previously, people used weaker methods, such as carefully locating each plug and socket, or in the very early days, looking at a wiring diagram. These techniques still work, but they are much more time consuming than just hooking things up where you can. The PC example is far from an isolated case. One of the hallmarks of good design is to arrange machinery so that the operator is constrained to do the right thing.

One can imagine a robot, capable of solving any problem whatsoever, that did so by applying a universal weak problem solving method to every problem it encountered. An outside observer would understand the robot's mind if the observer knew the problem solving method the robot used. Because humans solve a very wide variety of problems, it is not inconceivable that we also rely on some very general problem solving method. Therefore, it is reasonable to ask whether such methods can be identified.

This sort of thinking lead to Allen Newell and Herbert Simon (1972) to create the General Problem Solver (GPS) a program that was described briefly in chap. 3. To remind the reader briefly, the GPS represents problems as symbolic states of knowledge, analogous to the symbolic statement of the 'givens' and 'to prove' statements of geometry and algebra. The program then uses heuristic methods to move from state to state, until it finds a progression of states that lead from the original statement of the problem to the goal state.

To evaluate GPS as a theory of human thought, Newell and Simon and their colleagues (1972) asked people to talk aloud as they solved problems. An attempt was made to compare the step-by-step behavior of the program with the comments a person made. This technique, which is called *protocol analysis*, has led to substantial insights about problem solving. However issues in interpretation of verbal comments, and questions about their reliability, have kept protocol analysis of becoming an adequate test of programs as psychological models. In addition, the GPS model of problem solving as searching through states of knowledge often requires that the problem solver hold a great deal of information in some programming analog of working memory. Because working memory is a weak spot in human information processing, it seems unlikely that we rely heavily on it during complex problem solving. Finally, observational studies have shown that when people solve problems they rely a great deal on domain-specific (strong) techniques. This contrasts to GPS's reliance on the weak method of searching through a space of knowledge states.

Because of these objections, it cannot be said that the GPS program, in its entirety, models human problem solving. However, bits and pieces of the principles used to develop and test GPS have found their way into virtually every theory of problem solving proposed since 1970.

An alternative weak problem solving method is to use formal logic. We want to distinguish, though, between logic as an inference system and the techniques that are used to solve logic problems. We are interested in the techniques. One of them is searching a space of knowledge states, either as GPS or some other similar procedure does. Logic also allows a different procedure, called *model evaluation*. Model evaluation was introduced during the discussion of categorical reasoning, in chap. 9. It also applies outside of categorization, when we reason about the implications of statements like:

1. *If the Seattle football team wins the Super Bowl then there will be a celebration in Pioneer Square on Fat Tuesday.*
2. *There will be a celebration in Pioneer Square on Fat Tuesday.*
3. *Can we conclude that the Seattle football team won the Super Bowl?*

(The answer to the question is no.) According to Johnson-Laird's (1993) *mental models* theory, people solve problems like this one by trying to imagine all possible 'worlds'(*models*) in which the premises (statements 1 and 2) would be true, and then determining whether or not the conclusion (statement 3) is true in each of these worlds. Therefore a logical problem should be difficult if it either demands a large number of models or is worded in such a way as to make model construction difficult. Mental model theory does a reasonably good job of predicting the relative difficulty of different types of logical problems, and of explaining why two different wordings of the same logical problem can vary considerably in difficulty.

As we have noted, logical problems could be attacked either by an inference-drawing program, such as GPS, or by the mental models approach. It is hard to say which is correct, because human problem solving displays a great deal of variety. There are strong individual differences in the way that people attack logical problems. Consistency is not always found within an individual. The same person may sometimes use a models approach, sometimes a derivational approach, and sometimes attempt to reason from real-world knowledge about the problem cover story, without attempting logical analysis at all. For instance, if a citizen of Seattle were given the 'Super Bowl' problem presented above, the Seattlite might well say that he knew that there was a Fat Tuesday (Mardi Gras) celebration in Pioneer Square every year, and that the football team had never (as of 2001) even appeared in the Super Bowl, so the conclusion must be false. That is correct, but the respondent would not be playing the mathematical logic game.

The observed eclecticism in choice of problem solving methods is consistent with the blackboard architecture model of human information processing as described in chap. 3. According to this model thought is driven by pattern recognition. When a person is presented with a surface description of a problem productions (pattern -> action pairs) relevant to the surface description will be activated. If they trigger forward problem solving, then fine. At the same time, and often depending on the way that the problem is described, productions related to general problem solving methods, such as developing a symbolic description of a problem, may also be activated. Depending on the context, either the local (strong) or general (weak) production systems may carry the burden of problem solving. From the viewpoint of those who wish to create psychological theories, the resulting hodge-podge of problem solving behaviors is an annoyance. From the viewpoint of a person doing the problem solving, maintaining consistency in reasoning is usually less important than finding a solution.

Chapter 10/2Deduction *contains a more detailed discussion of these issues.*

10.3 Analogical Reasoning

Reasoning by deduction can be justified by a well-developed logical theory of what constitutes a valid argument. Reasoning by analogy is more intuitive. In spite of its informality, analogical reasoning is very common. Modern day American English is rife with analogical references, especially ones based on sports. Business leaders will say that "It's the bottom of the ninth," a baseball term for the end of the game, to refer to a commercial situation in which final decisions must be made. Analogies are found in other places as well. Indeed, American and English reliance on case law and precedent is a form of analogy. The present case is decided on the basis of its resemblance to another, previously decided, case.

People do much better in solving problems for which they have an analogy than they do when they attempt to solve problems without such support. Experimental studies have shown that providing an analogy can increase problem solving rates from less than 10% to more than 50%. Historical studies reveal that analogical arguments have been used to support major decisions, in situations ranging from research in physics to choosing foreign policies.

A few term descriptions are necessary before we proceed. The problem to be solved is referred to as the *target* problem. The analogical problem is called the *base*. The target and base problems are typically about something (e.g., business decisions are about financial, personnel, and policy matters; baseball decisions are about coaches, players, and game strategies). These are called the *surface elements* of a problem. The surface elements are tied together in a *relational structure*, that links the elements to each other. Causal relations appear to be particularly important.

A good analogy is one that establishes a mapping between surface elements of the base and target structure in such a way that the mapping shows how the known relational structure of the base problem applies to the target problem. Consider the fairly frequent term in late 1990s business English, in which a failing firm is described as seeking a White Knight. This is an analogy to the many stories in which a king, facing intractable problems, seeks a hero in white armor who comes riding in to slay the dragon. What the business is really seeking is an outside investor who will pay off its debts. And in both cases, appropriate rewards are expected: either a beautiful princess or a generous stock arrangement.

To reason by analogy a potential base has to be retrieved from memory. It then has to be aligned with the target. Finally, the relations uncovered in the base problem have to be applied to the target situation. These steps can conflict. Similarity between surface elements seems to guide the effort to locate a base problem, while similarity between relational structures determines the usefulness of the base problem once it has been uncovered. These two effects can combine to produce interesting results. In one experiment, college students who had some training in history read a story describing how a powerful, dictatorial nation was threatening a small neighbor. The students were asked whether the United States should intervene. When the conflict was described as taking place in (apparently) a European context, most students drew an analogy to the events prior to World War II and thought that the U.S. should intervene. When the conflict was described as taking place between two tropical nations, many students drew an analogy to the Vietnam war, and said the U.S. should not intervene.

The same principles have been illustrated, and elaborated on, in many other experiments. All of these studies show that analogical reasoning appears to be much easier to do than deductive inference. At the same time, the studies show how analogical reasoning can be ambiguous, for there can be arguments over the right analogy, and how the different ways that the target–base mapping is constructed can lead to different interpretations of the target problem, even when the target and base problems are the same.

> *This brief discussion only touches on some of the issues involved in analogical reasoning. For a more complete discussion with extended examples, see* Chapter 4/3 AnalogicalReasoning.

10.4 Schematic Reasoning

Schematic reasoning occurs when a problem solver classifies a situation as being an example of a certain class of problems, and then applies procedures that are suitable for the class to the problem at hand. The application can be so automatic that it approaches stereotyped behavior. Although this makes schematic reasoning seem mindless, it is not. Schematic reasoning has been observed to be characteristic of expert physicists and mathematicians, people whom we certainly think of as being good problem solvers.

Both physicists and mathematicians attempt to solve a problem in their field by classifying it as a problem of a type for whom a solution method is known. They then apply the solution method. If the solution is not found, the expert tries a new classification and a new solution method. This sort of behavior contrasts with that of novice problem solvers in the same field. Novices rely more on general (weak) problem solving methods.

Schematic reasoning is certainly not limited to physics and mathematics. Domain specific schematic reasoning has been observed for behaviors as varied as comprehending a radio broadcast of a baseball game and determining the appropriate disposition of shoplifting cases. The expert in this or that field is often a person who has learned to use a great many domain-specific schema, whereas the novice is a person who has to work out each solution as if it were a new problem. A second distinction between experts and novices is that experts are much better than novices at recognizing when a particular schema applies. This appears to be because the experts have learned to look at problems in their field in a way that encourages an abstract description, which then can be matched to the abstract description of a problem-solving schema. Novices tend to become enmeshed in the surface features of the particular problem.

Some schematic reasoning represents an intermediate stage between strongly constrained, domain-specific sorts of reasoning just referred to and the weakly constrained general problem solving methods associated with logic and mathematics. We see a good example of this in logical problem solving. The logical relation of implication can be broken down into at least two intermediate schema; a *causal* interpretation of A implies B as A causes B, and a *permission* interpretation, such as, "Observing that someone did X implies that the person had permission to do X." When a problem permits either of these interpretations people do much better than when they have to deal with abstract problems involving implication. Similar schema have been observed in elementary mathematics. Grade school children readily understand *transfer schema*, as in "Mary had five marbles. Then John gave her four. How many does Mary have?" even when they have trouble with the abstract mathematics.

As was the case in analogical reasoning, schematic reasoning forces problem solvers to solve the access and alignment problems. Both can be difficult. Access is surprisingly domain-specific. It is a commonplace observation that students can be taught (physical and mathematical) schema in school, and then fail to apply them outside of the school setting. In fact, schema learned in one class may not transfer to another, even when the application is straightforward to an outsider. Solving the alignment problem requires that the problem solver establish a correspondence between elements and relations in the schema and elements and relations in the current problem. This can also be surprisingly difficult. Possibly the most well known example is in mathematics. High school students find it extraordinarily difficult to move from word problems to a general algebraic statement (i.e., to map from situation to schema), even in cases where the students can work out numerical solutions to the problems.

Schema related to causation are of particular interest. Logically a causal relation such as A *causes* B can be represented by an implication relation, A *implies* B. This relation is satisfied providing that B is true whenever A is true, and can only be falsified by showing a case in which A is true and B is false. Call this the *syntactic* constraint on causation. When people reason about causation they introduce three additional *pragmatic* constraints. The *temporal* constraint is that A must precede B in time. The *mechanism* constraint is that there must be some understood mechanism that explains why A must be followed by B. Finally, the *control* constraint requires that the presence of A must not covary with some other factor A, that might also be a cause of B. The control constraint is sometimes seen as a hallmark of scientific reasoning, for it dictates the logic of the controlled study, in which the probability of B, given A (e.g., the probability of resisting a cold, given that one has taken vitamins) is systematically compared to the probability of B, given ~A (the probability of resisting a cold, given that vitamins have not been taken).

To detect causation, it is necessary to observe how appearances of A and B covary. In the typical case, problem solvers only consider covariance over what they consider *focal events*. For instance, when discussing whether or not discarded cigarettes are a major cause of forest fires, no one suggests examining whether cigarettes have caused forest fires in Antarctica, where forests are nonexistent, or in a rain forest in the winter when it is difficult to start a fire intentionally. Therefore, if you wish to understand how a person reasons about causation you must have some way of understanding what he or she regards as the focal events for the situation under discussion. Once again, we see that domain-specific considerations have been introduced, rather than relying solely on a logic, a weak problem solving technique.

Where do schema come from? Experimental studies and observations of problem solving in the field are converging on two findings. Although some schema can be acquired simply by being told about them, schema can also be acquired by extending analogical problem solving to the use of the same analogy in several settings. Having seen a few different uses of analogy, problem solvers begin to grasp the general principle embodied in the schema. However, the general principle is only appreciated if the learner reflects on his or her experience. Studies on the way that students use analogies and work through example problems have shown that there are wide individual differences in the extent to which people reflect on what they are doing. Some seem to simply plug the analogy into the problem, whereas others reflect on the general principles involved.

> Chapter 10/4SchematicReasoning *extends this discussion considerably. The section includes descriptions of experiments on schematic reasoning and an analysis of historical cases in which schematic reasoning was displayed.*

10.5 Schematic Reasoning and Analogies in Education

Education is a place where applications of cognitive psychology ought to bear fruit. In the case of schema-based reasoning, it has. Schema-based reasoning has been used to develop a successful remedial mathematics program for college students. In this program, the students are explicitly taught to recognize situations in which certain schematic problem solving methods can be used. A program for teaching introductory physics (facet-based instruction), has taken another approach. The teacher assumes that students enter the class with schema (facets) that are either limited or actualy erroneous. For instance, many students have an Aristotelian view of motion, believing that objects naturally come to rest unless something keeps pushing them. This contrasts with the Newtonian view that objects in motion remain in motion unless a force is imposed on them. The teacher engages students in discussions that reveal the facets they have prior to instruction. Subsequently, the teacher tailors instruction to move the students toward the facets (schema) that experts use to analyze physics problems.

> *The educational programs are described in more detail in* Chapter 5/5Education.

10.6 A Theoretical Summary

The problem solving literature is chaotic, as different investigators have studied different problems for different reasons. Some of this chaos may be inevitable, as problem solving is at best a fuzzy category of behavior. Nevertheless, there is some order to the chaos, and it can be summarized with a model of how problem solving may occur.

The model described in the main text emphasizes concreteness. In it, the first step in problem solving is to see if the problem has been presented before. If it has, assert the new solution. Next, search for an analogical problem and use it to guide solution. If an analogy cannot be found, attempt to fit the problem into a previously acquired schema, using that schema to guide problem solving. During the searches for analogies and schema, it may be necessary to redescribe the problem. Finally, and only as a last resort, apply weak problem solving methods, such as GPS or model-based logical reasoning.

The guiding principle for the model, and I believe for human reasoning, is that our minds are organized for memory, not thought. Reasoning is a last resort, and there is nothing wrong with this. There are a very few contexts in which we place premiums on the elegant solution of new problems. We spend most of our time solving problems that are very much like ones we have encountered before.

Chapter 10/6Summary *contains a more expanded summary.*

11

Decision Making: Psychological Models of Choice

11.1 The Components of Decision Making

Decision making refers to the selection of a course of action from a set of alternatives. This topic is of interest to both economists and psychologists. Economists develop models to describe ideal choice behavior. These are called *normative* models. Psychologists are interested in *descriptive* models of how people actually behave. Some psychologists develop descriptive models by observing decision making in artificial but controlled laboratory studies. Others do so by conducting field studies of decision-making behavior in everyday life. Rather different views of decision making have emerged from these two approaches.

Decision makers have to predict the future. They do so by examining present evidence to infer future events. Two different philosophic views can be used. The *analytic* view is that the future is preordained, either by divine intervention or by mechanistic causal laws operating on the present state of the world. The *frequentist* view is that the future can only be determined probabilistically, so that all decision making is analogous to gambling. Although these views sound quite different, in practice they lead to similar normative models of behavior. People who take an analytic view can argue that they do not have complete confidence in their abilities to read the signs pointing to the future, and therefore the probability calculus is a useful way of expressing their subjective probability estimates. People who take a frequentist view bet that the future will be like the past, for they use past observations to estimate the probability of future events. (Weather prediction is a good example.) Frequentists do not think that the future is determined by some sort of cosmic roulette wheel. They do argue that their imperfect ability to observe the present forces them to accept a probabilistic view of the future.

In practice, decision making can be studied without inquiring into the decision maker's philosophic views about probability. It is important to know whether the decision maker's estimates of the probabilities of events conform to the mathematical definition of a probability measure. These are that (a) every imaginable event under consideration have a probability ranging from zero to one, (b) that the probabilities sum to one, and that (c) the probability of the combined observation, A and B, be equal to the probability that A occurs, multiplied by the probability that B occurs given that A has occurred. When these constraints are met, a person's probability estimates can be combined with their estimate of the worth of possible rewards to develop a model of rational decision making.

To do this, we have to consider the nature of a reward. Observations and, perhaps more influentially, compelling thought experiments, dating back to the 18th century, have shown that people do not behave in a way that would maximize the objective value of rewards for their actions. Instead they maximize the *utility* of a reward, where the utility is the subjective value of the reward for the decision maker involved. Utility is a psychological concept, and we shall consider several of its characteristics below. Most modern economic theory regards rational behavior as the behavior that would be displayed if a person makes choices between lotteries in such a way as to maximize the expected utility of the outcome.

See Chapter 11/1IntroductoryConcepts *for an expansion on these remarks.*

11.2 The Von Neumann-Morgenstern Approach: Expected Utility

Modern treatments of decision theory have been heavily influenced by the work of John Von Neumann and Oskar Morgenstern. They considered decision making as a choice between lotteries, where each lottery can be described by a prize, an alternate prize, and a probability of winning. Consider, for example, the classic lottery, in which a person purchases a ticket at cost $T, and has a chance of winning a prize $Z, with probability p, or else receiving nothing. This lottery can be described by (($Z-$T, p), (-$T, 1-p)). In actual lotteries the cost of the ticket is usually miniscule compared to the size of the prize, and p is very small. In business decisions, though, p may be high and $T may be within a few percentage points of $Z. To see this, consider the potential gain to a farmer of purchasing a new harvester that will function with probability p (which would probably be in excess of $.95) compared to the cost if the harvester broke down.

Von Neumann and Morgenstern argued that any *decision under risk* can be thought of as a gamble, akin to a lottery, in which the choice is between two or more 'lotteries.' They stated seven axioms that they believed characterized rational choices between lotteries. The mathematical forms of the axioms are stated in the main text. In words, these axioms are as follows:

Ordering. The decision maker has transitive preferences for each of the possible prizes.

Compound Lotteries. Consider a lottery, involving two prizes and some probability of winning the more valuable prizes, and a two-stage lottery in which the first stage is a lottery whose prizes are tickets of entry into one of two second-stage lotteries, each involving the original two prizes. The decision maker is indifferent between a one- and a two-stage lottery, providing that the probabilities of ultimately winning each prize are identical in each lottery.

Continuity. Every lottery has a fixed price that an individual is willing to pay to enter. This fixed price must be intermediate between the most and least valuable prizes in the lottery.

Substitutability. A decision maker is indifferent between a lottery and a second lottery in which prizes of equivalent value are substituted for the prizes in the original lottery.

Choice is Independent of Irrelevant Alternatives. Suppose that a decision maker prefers alternative O_1 to alternative O_2. This preference is not changed if the decision maker is informed that an alternative, O_3, is available, but O_3 is not preferred to O_1 or O_2.

Transitivity. Choices between lotteries are transitive.

Monotonicity. Given a choice between two lotteries, with the same prizes but different probabilities of winning, a decision maker will always choose the lottery with the highest probability of winning.

Von Neumann and Morgenstern (1947) proved that if these axioms are satisfied for a set of gambles involving possible outcomes, $\{O_1 \ldots O_k\}$ then it is possible to assign numbers (utilities) $\{u(O_1) \ldots u(O_k)\}$ to the outcomes such that the lottery chosen is always the one with the highest *expected utility*, where expected utility of a lottery is defined as the sum of the utilities of the possible outcomes, each weighted by its probability of occurrence. Generalizing the terminology, Von Neumann and Morgenstern (1947) defined a *decision under risk* as a situation in which a person is faced with a choice between two or more alternatives, and where the consequences of each choice are only known up to a probability distribution. This description applies to such disparate situations as an investor's deciding what stocks to purchase and a football coach's deciding whether to tell his team to run or pass the ball. In each case, the individual choices can be looked on, abstractly, as lotteries. Therefore, preferences amongst lotteries can serve as a model for decision making under risk. If the axioms correctly describe a rational decision maker, then a rational decision maker should always choose the alternative (lottery) with the highest expected utility.

If one wishes to use the Von Neumann and Morgenstern model as a descriptive model of behavior, the *parameterization* problem must be solved. Utility values must be assigned to all outcomes in the decision making situation, and subjective probabilities must be found for the occurrence of all events on which the relevant gambles depend. To take a whimsical case, suppose that we wished to determine whether a fairytale hero would accept the challenge to fight a dragon, thus winning a kingdom and princess. Subjective utility theory requires that we know the hero's utility for the kingdom, the princess, and the (dis)utility of death by dragon. We also need to find out the hero's subjective probability that he is going to defeat the dragon. Furthermore, the two estimates must be independent. The hero's subjective probability that he will kill the dragon must not depend on the utility of kingdom and princess. More generally, the assumption that subjective probability estimates are independent of the utility of the associated rewards is a major psychological assumption.

Suppose the decision maker behaves in such a way that it can be proven that it is impossible to parameterize the utility and subjective probability functions. (Note that a proof is required. Stating you have been unable to find such functions is not enough.) In this case, the decision-maker must not be acting rationally, in the sense defined by the Von Neumann and Morgenstern axioms. What can be done?

Deviations from the subjective expected utility model could arise in two ways. It might be that the person doing the analysis does not understand how the decision maker perceives the problem. Apparently irrational behavior may become rational when one realizes what the decision maker's view of the rewards and alternative actions are. This is particularly true if the observer chooses to analyze a person's behavior in a single decision making situation, whereas the decision-maker sees the situation as being embedded in a social context. It may make short-term sense for a business operation to take every possible advantage of its customers and suppliers, but it does not make long-term sense to acquire a reputation for doing so. To the extent to which this sort of consideration is true, normative decision theory (and any other theory of rational behavior) cannot be a description of behavior until it is augmented by a theory of the decision-maker's perception of the situation.

An alternative possibility is that normative decision making, even in its augmented version, is not descriptive because the behavior required by the normative theory makes impossible demands on human information processing. If this is true descriptive theories will not be weakened versions of normative theory. The normative theory has to be replaced by models of decision making based on fundamentally different assumptions than the maximization of expected utility.

There is an extensive literature on ways the Von Neumann and Morgenstern approach might be augmented to become a descriptive theory, examined in the next section. We also look at the argument for building a descriptive theory that is almost separate from the normative one.

For further details of the normative theory see Chapter 11/2NormativeDecisionMaking.

11.3 Augmenting Expected Utility Theory

Efforts to change expected utility theory into a descriptive theory have to do two things; establish the form of the utility-objective wealth and subjective probability-objective probability functions, and explain why they take the form that they do.

Efforts to modify utility theory have to deal with some well known apparent paradoxes. People will purchase tickets to enter a lottery although the price of the ticket exceeds the expected winnings. This is called *risk seeking* behavior, the decision maker prefers a lottery to a sure thing (keeping the price of the ticket) that equals or exceeds the expected value of the lottery. Risk seeking behavior is logical if the utility function for money is positively accelerated. However, the same person who buys a lottery ticket will purchase insurance, where the price of the insurance exceeds the expected value of a loss. This is *risk aversive* behavior, that can be explained by assuming that the utility function for money is negatively accelerated. There is a simple utility function explanation for both risk seeking and risk aversive behavior, but not for both simultaneously.

The observations just presented are based on common sense. Some laboratory studies have shown another puzzling phenomenon that appears to contradict the lottery insurance case. In laboratory studies, participants (often college students) were offered choices between a sure gain; a gamble between no gain or a large one, and a certain loss; a gamble between no loss or a large loss. When the choice involves gain, people generally choose the sure gain; when the choice involves loss, most people take the gamble. Once again, we see risk seeking and risk avoidance behavior, but this time it is reversed; people are risk aversive in a positive situation and risk seeking in a negative one. At this point, we have two paradoxes. The laboratory and the field observations, taken singly, are inconsistent with theory that states that utility is either a positively or negatively accelerated function of value throughout all ranges of values. Furthermore, the laboratory and field observations are consistent with each other.

Prospect theory modifies utility theory to deal with this sort of situation. According to prospect theory, the utility of an outcome is determined by the difference between the value of the outcome and the value of what the decision maker considers a reasonable return in the situation. This is called the *prospect point*. Prospect theory further assumes that the utility function for money is positively accelerated below the prospect point, negatively accelerated above it, and that the degree of departure from linearity is greater below than it is above the prospect point. (This situation is presented graphically in the main text.) These assumptions are sufficient to deal with the laboratory findings, for they predict risk aversion for a gain situation and risk seeking in a loss situation. An additional assumption is required to account for the lottery insurance paradox, that for very large rewards and/or penalties the utility function changes so that it is positively and negatively accelerated above and below an inflection point, instead of below and above the prospect point. To put this in terms of our insurance lottery example, people buy insurance against severe to catastrophic losses, not against minor damages. Similarly, acceptable gambles hold the promise of great gains, rather than modest ones.

Given these assumptions, prospect theory does a good job of predicting when people will be risk seeking and when they will be risk aversive. To do so, it is important to know whether the decision-maker sees the situation as one of avoiding loss or achieving gain. In some laboratory studies, decision-makers have been switched from risk seeking to risk aversion in the same objective situation by describing the situation in a way that emphasizes potential gains or potential losses. This is called the *framing* phenomenon, a purely psychological augmentation of utility theory.

DECISION MAKING

A descriptive theory has to parameterize subjective probability and utility. A well-established finding is that people tend to overestimate the probability of infrequent events and underestimate the probability of frequent ones. This alone would be sufficient to explain the insurance lottery paradox, for a purchaser would overestimate the likelihood of a catastrophe and of winning a lottery. A rather complex mathematical equation (see the main text) has been developed that provides a reasonable approximation of the degree of underestimation and overestimation.

The equation describes the relation between objective and subjective probability estimates, but it does not explain how the subjective estimates come to be. This question has been approached in two different ways. One is to consider how people change their estimates of the probability of a situation as they gather more information about it. Formally, imagine a person who is trying to choose a hypothesis from a finite set of possible hypotheses. Each hypothesis specifies a probability for each of a finite set of possible outcomes of observations. Imagine further that observations are taken one at a time, and the (subjective) probability of each hypothesis is recalculated every time an observation is taken. What is the appropriate procedure for readjusting the subjective probabilities of each hypothesis?

The optimal procedure, *Bayes Theorem*, was discovered in the 18th century. This theorem and the reasoning behind it are at the basis of much of modern statistics. Experimental studies show that people deviate from Bayes theorem in two systematic ways. First, they undervalue evidence that shows that a certain hypothesis is not correct. This causes conservative adjustment; people will maintain hypotheses in the face of contradictory evidence. Second, people fail to consider adequately *base rate* evidence. That is, hypotheses with low probabilities may be overvalued if the evidence seems to fit them better than it fits a hypothesis with high initial probability, but that does not fit the evidence quite as well. To capture the spirit of this issue, imagine that you are walking along a wooded stream and you see a paw print in the mud. It may look exactly like the picture of a wolf's paw print in a tracking book, but unless you are in the outer areas of Canada or Alaska, it is far more likely to be from another hiker's large dog.

Listing deviations from the behavior prescribed by Bayes' theorem provides a descriptive statement of how people behave, but does not explain why they behave in this way. *Support theory* is an attempt to do this. According to support theory, people estimate the probability of a hypothesis by evaluating the evidence for each of two competing hypotheses (the *support*), and then calculate the odds by taking the ratio of the relevant supports. That is, for two hypotheses, A and B, supports $S(A)$ and $S(B)$, and *subjective* probabilities, $Pr(A)$ and $Pr(B)$,

Pr(A):Pr(B) = S(A):S(B).

A second assumption of support theory is that when a particular hypothesis is signaled out for special attention, people think about it more and thus, find more support than they would if the hypothesis were to be considered along with other mutually exclusive hypotheses. This means that support is *subadditive* in the following sense. Let compound hypothesis A ∪ B be the hypothesis "either A or B is true" and assume that A and B are mutually exclusive (i.e., both cannot be true). The subadditive assumption is that:

S(A ∪ B) ≤ S(A) + S(B).

For instance, suppose that four tennis players, A, B, C, and D were playing in a tennis tournament. An expert is asked to estimate the probability that player A will win the tournament, then player B, then player C, and then D. The expert is then asked whether any of these four players will win. According to the subadditive hypothesis, the sum of the individual estimates may not equal the compound estimate.

Support theory was initially proposed in the 1990s, and has yet to be given an extensive evaluation. (Experiments where it has been evaluated do indicate that it gives an adequate account of behavior.) However, it has raised a problem. According to support theory, subjective probability estimates may not satisfy the constraints of a probability measure. When this happens, the probability calculus no longer applies, so much of the mathematical backing for the normative theory of decision making collapses.

This raises a profound issue. Does von Neumann and Morgenstern's (1947) use of choices between lotteries apply to actual decision making? It certainly does to decision making in laboratory situations, because those situations were constructed to be lotteries. In the world outside the laboratory, things may be much different.

The mathematical basis for the remarks made here, together with several examples, can be found in Chapter 11/3AugmentingNormativeTheory.

11.4 Replacing Normative Theory

Shortly after von Neumann and Morgenstern (1947) published their statement of utility theory, Herbert Simon (1955) criticized their proposal on

DECISION MAKING

the grounds that their lottery model of decision making was unrealistic. The lottery model assumes that all available alternatives and consequences are known to the decision maker at the time that a course of action is chosen. In practice, decision makers often do not know what are the alternatives until they take their first, tentative actions. Simon (1955) also pointed out that the von Neumann and Morgenstern approach (1947) disregarded the need to choose actions within a prescribed time, often without as much information as the utility maximization model assumed, and disregarded the cost involved in examining multiple alternatives. Simon argued that in practice what people do is to look for the first alternative that seems to provide a satisfactory reward. Therefore, people should be described as *satisficing* expected utility rather than maximizing it.

Simon's arguments derived as much from his studies of organizational behavior as considerations of decision making in the abstract. Since Simon's (1955) proposals a number of investigators have studied decision making outside the laboratory, in settings ranging from couples deciding on family planning to national leaders deciding whether to start a war. In general, satisficing seems to be more descriptive than utility maximization. However, an even more radical approach may be called for. It is usually possible to cast actual decision making into the language of classical decision theory, but doing so fails to capture much of the flavor of the observed behavior. Instead of determining and weighing alternatives, as if they were lotteries, real decision makers concentrate on finding what seems to be a satisfactory alternative, developing a plan that depicts how events will unfold if this alternative is taken, and being ready to change alternatives if things seem to be turning out in a different way than had been anticipated.

Three factors seem to govern everyday decision making. One is the importance of people's internal representations of themselves, others, and the situation. These are used to determine what the permissible alternatives are and what their consequences are believed to be. Sometimes physically possible, objectively attractive actions will be ruled out because they conflict with the decision-maker's personal image. A notable example was then President Kennedy's refusal to order an unannounced air strike on Cuba during the 1962 Cuban Missile Crisis. The argument for not doing so was that this would be inconsistent with America's image of itself. The second principle is the importance of schematic reasoning. Important decisions are generally left to people who have a great deal of domain-specific experience. They draw on this experience to decide what to do. Often, the decision is made because it is the decision dictated by relevant schema, not because it is the best of several evaluated alternatives. Also, there are not very many cases in which final decisions are made. Decisions are made, and then re-evaluated as new information becomes available. None of these considerations are part of the lottery model of decision making.

Medical decision making can be used to illustrate all these points. In the abstract, medical decision making can be cast as a choice between lotteries; different diagnoses have varying probabilities of being correct, and different treatments offer different probability distributions over the available set of outcomes. Indeed, there are hundreds, if not thousands, of laboratory studies in which medical decision-making is used as a cover story to study how people choose amongst lotteries. Although the participants are often college students, sometimes they are actual physicians or patients.

Whoever the participants are, it is unlikely that such studies are simulations of real medical decision making. Psychologists who have observed physicians making diagnoses and treating real cases have found that physicians behave like problem solvers, as discussed in chap. 10. They apply schematic reasoning, seek causal explanations for their observations, and shift readily from forward to backward reasoning when appropriate. They do not think of themselves as gamblers choosing between lotteries.

Paradoxically, it can be argued that those who decide medical policy, such as health maintenance organizations and insurance companies, ought to regard alternative treatments as a choice between lotteries.

Chapter 11/4–5OutsideTheLaboratory *expands on the deficiencies of the von Neumann and Morgenstern approach as a basis for developing descriptive decision making theories that apply outside the laboratory. The section contains several examples, including an extended discussion of medical decision making.*

12

Where Have We Been and Where Are We Going?

Cognitive psychology has made substantial leaps forward in our knowledge of thought. The greatest progress has been made in research of the study of memory and visual perception. We are moving rapidly toward understanding the link between biological mechanisms of the brain and information processing models of the mind. In each case, understanding the biological mechanisms depends on having the information processing models, so cognitive psychologists can be justifiably proud of their contribution.

In the near future, continued studies on the interaction between mind and brain are certain to continue. It is hard to see how progress can fail, given current technological advances that enable us, quite literally, to see the brain act as the mind thinks. Modern imaging techniques, the untangling of the human genome, and other advances outside of psychology may be as important to the study of cognition as the invention of the microscope was to the study of biology. The barrier between studies of the brain and studies of the mind has been breached, and this is a very good thing.

Progress has also been made toward understanding how the mind works at the representational level. Present day models of deductive inference and analogical reasoning are well advanced beyond those in the textbooks of the 1950s. Nevertheless, there is a certain disquiet. I, and possibly other knowledgeable observers, have a vague feeling that we should have done better. The contributions of cognitive psychology to education and industry have been less than they should have been.

Cognitive psychology is partly to blame. From its inception, cognitive psychology has focused on the capabilities of the individual problem solver, with little concern for an individual's motivation or social and technological setting within which problem solving takes place. In practice, cognition is a highly social act, very much guided by the motivations of the thinkers. This observation is not an attack on all that has been learned from laboratory studies of thought. Such attacks are naïve, for a great deal has been learned. However, further advances in understanding thinking at the representational level will require breaking down the distinction between studying the individual mind and studying the social and technological settings in which that mind is used.

For expansion on these comments, see Chapter 12/The Future. *The discussion includes a brief listing of potential advances in cognitive psychology in the next 50 years.*

Author Index

A

Anderson, J. R., 32, 51

B

Baddeley, A., 20, 21, 22, 58, 75, 83
Bartlett, F., 53
Biederman, I., 79, 80

C

Chomsky, N., 2, 45, 73, 74, 100
Crick, F., 5

D

Descartes, R., 2

E

Ebbinghaus, H., 52, 53, 61

F

Freud, S., 52, 67

H

Hebb, D. O., 41, 42

J

James, W., 15, 52, 56
Johnson-Laird, P., 128, 139

K

Kintsch, W., 104
Kosslyn, S., 83

M

Marr, D., 78, 79, 80
Morgenstern, O., 148, 149, 150, 151, 154, 155

N

Newell, A., 2, 25, 28, 29, 138, 139

P

Piaget, J., 73, 74

S

Simon, H., 2, 5, 25, 28, 29, 138, 139, 154, 155
Sternberg, S., 18

T

Tversky, A., 123, 124

V

Von Neumann, J., 148, 149, 150, 151, 154, 155

W

Wagenaar, W., 72, 73

Subject Index

A

Abstract informational processing level, 3
Amnesia, anterograde, 17
Artifacts, 93–96
Artificial intelligence, 25
Audition, 12

B

Blackboard models, 20, 25, 27–29, 30–33
    learning, 31–33, 39–42
Bottoms-up cue, 77
Brain-mind relations, 5–7
Brain system, 3

C

Categorical reasoning, 107–111
    characteristic feature, 108
    defining feature, 108–129
    feature-based, 110
    nonspacial madels, 123–125
    reasoning by inheritance, 109
    semantic space, 110, 118
    spatial models, 121–122
Categorical reasoning for conscious strategies, 127–136
    categorization based on knowledge, 130–133
        interaction/essence views, 131–132
        natural kinds, 130–131
        standard model, 130
    conceptual coherence, 133–134
    propositional categories, 127–130
        conservative focusing, 129
    relations between concepts, 134–136
Cognitive neuroscience, 6, 15
Computer programs, 1–5
Conceptual issues, 29–31
Configural representations, 76
Connectionist modeling, 25, 35–36
    computations in neural networks, 36–39
    constraint networks, 42–44
    evaluation, 47–50
    illustrative applications, 44–46
    learning, 39–42
    variable binding problem, 46–47
Consciousness, 12–15, 22–23
    long term memory, 12–13, 17–19
    short term memory, 13–14, 17–19
Context effects, 71

D

Decision making, 147–148
    augmenting expected utility theory, 151–154
    replacing normative theory, 154–156
    Von Neumann-Morganstern approach, 148–151, 154–156
    axioms, 149
Depth of processing, 72–73
Description matching, 81

SUBJECT INDEX

E

Encoding specificity, 72–73
Evolutionary psychology, 73
External information processing, 9–10
    channel capacity, 9–10
    cybernetic principle, 9–10

G

Geons, 79–80
GPS, 28–29, 30, 32

H

Human-sensory-perceptual system, 5

I

Imagery, 75, 83–85
Information processing system, 3–4, 5, 53

L

Language, 98–100, 101–103
    generative grammar theory, 99–100
    mentalese, 99–100, 105–106
    syntax, 98–99, 100–103
    transformational rules, 100

M

Memory, 51–55
    brain imaging, 54
    encoding stage, 51, 53
    experiments, 54–55
    retrieval stage, 51, 53, 54
    storage, 51, 54
Memory, physical basis of, 15
    hippocampus, 16
Memory storage, 16–17
Memory systems, 55–68
    dual coding hypothesis, 56, 61–63
    emotional, 63–64
    episodic–semantic, 56, 60–61
    Freud, 55, 66–68
    implicit long term, 64–66
    long term declarative, 56, 59–60
    short term declarative, 56, 58
    short term implicit, 56, 58–59
Models of knowledge organization, 111
    behavioral violations of spatial models, 123
Multidimensional Scaling (MDS), 118–119
    multiplicative similarity model, 116–118
    spatial models for organizing information, 111–113
    construction, 113–116
    defining class, 119–120

P

Parameter setting, 73–74
Perception, 83–85
Philosophy of cognitive psychology, 2, 5–8
    brain states, 2–3, 54
Pragmatic dualism, 2–3

Probabilistic categorization, 125–126
Production system approach, 27–28
Production system programming, 25–27, 30, 33
Psycholinguistic approaches, 101–103
    short term memory, 102

R

Reasoning, 137–146
    analogical, 141–142
    deduction and inference, 138–140
    schematic, 142–145
        in education, 145
    theoretical summary, 145–146
Reductionism, 2–3, 8
Representational system, 3–4, 6–8
Route representations, 76

S

Schema, 33–34, 53
Source amnesia, 71
Spatial orientation, 75, 81–82, 85
    individual differences, 92–93
    surrounds, 88–92
    wayfinding, 85–86
Studies of primary memory, 17–22

T

Top down cues, 77

U

Understanding discourse, 103–105

V

Venus de Milo, 79
Visual perception, 75
Visual reasoning, 81–93
    spatial rotation, 81–82
    visualization, 81–82
Visual system, 10–12

```
BF          Hunt, Earl B.
311
.H78        Precis of thoughts on
2002           thought.


                                          46207
$29.95
                    DATE
```

BAKER & TAYLOR